Skills for Study

LEVEL 1

Craig Fletcher   Blair Matthews

Series editor: Ian Smallwood

CAMBRIDGE

CAMBRIDGE
UNIVERSITY PRESS

University Printing House, Cambridge CB2 8BS, United Kingdom

One Liberty Plaza, 20th Floor, New York, NY 10006, USA

477 Williamstown Road, Port Melbourne, VIC 3207, Australia

314–321, 3rd Floor, Plot 3, Splendor Forum, Jasola District Centre, New Delhi – 110025, India

79 Anson Road, #06–04/06, Singapore 079906

Cambridge University Press is part of the University of Cambridge.

It furthers the University's mission by disseminating knowledge in the pursuit of
education, learning and research at the highest international levels of excellence.

Information on this title: www.cambridge.org

First published 2012

20 19 18 17 16 15 14 13 12 11 10 9 8 7 6 5 4

Printed in Malaysia by Vivar

A catalogue record for this publication is available from the British Library

ISBN 978-1-107-63544-9 Paperback

Acknowledgements

The authors and publishers acknowledge the following sources of copyright
material and are grateful for the permissions granted. While every effort has
been made, it has not always been possible to identify the sources of all the
material used, or to trace all copyright holders. If any omissions are brought
to our notice, we will be happy to include the appropriate acknowledgements
on reprinting.

Loughborough University for the text on pp. 20–21 'Deep and surface
approaches to learning' written by Houghton, W. (2004). *Engineering Subject
Centre Guide: Learning and Teaching Theory for Engineering Academics*,
Loughborough University: HEA, Engineering Subject Centre. Reproduced
with permission;

Dr James E. Witte for the text on p. 40 'Learning styles and students'
attitudes toward the use of technology in higher and adult education classes'
written by Cox, T. (2008). *Institute for Learning Styles Journal*, 1, 1–13.
Journal Editor, Dr James E. Witte. Reproduced with permission;

Professor Antony D'Emanuele for the text on pp. 54, 55 'The internet: a
global communication tool' adapted from D'Emanuele, A. (1995). The
internet: a global communication tool, *International Pharmacy Journal*, 9
(2), pp. 68–72. Reproduced with permission;

Dr Sonia Livingstone for the text on p. 53, 58–59 'How children use
the media' and 'Trends in media use among young people', based on
Livingstone, Sonia & Bovill, Moira (1999) *Young People, New Media: Report
of the Research Project Children, Young People and the Changing Media
Environment*. Reproduced with permission;

Belbin Associates, UK for the text on p. 63 'Team role descriptions' adapted
from *Team Roles at Work*, written by Meredith Belbin, 1993. Reproduced
with permission;

Text on pp. 77, 83 from 'Preparing for The Big Chill', *The Spectator*, 289.
Retrieved from http://www.spectator.co.uk/essays/10104/prepare-for-the-big-
chill.thtml/Kenny, A. (2002, June);

Sara Wittenberg for the text on pp. 101–102 'Environmental dangers of plastic
bags' from *Environmental dangers of plastic bags*,
www.suite101.com, 6 June 2009. Reproduced with permission;

Ministry of Social Development, New Zealand for the chart on p. 138 'Health
expectancy at birth by gender, 1996, 2001 and 2006' and for the text on pp.
139–140 'The health expectancy situation in New Zealand' adapted from
Ministry of Social Development. (2010). *Social Report 2010*. Wellington: New
Zealand Ministry of Social Development. Reproduced with permission;

Macmillan Publishers Ltd for the text on pp. 144–146 'Maintaining a healthy
lifestyle into old age' adapted from *College English Creative Reading (Book 3)*
written by C. Green. Reprinted with permission; Anup Shah for the text on
pp. 187–191 'A brief Introduction to climate change' adapted from *Climate
Change and Global Warming*, www.globalissues.org. Reproduced with
permission.

Photo acknowledgements

p. 4 1 ©Chris Schmidt/istockphoto.com, 2 ©Muharrem Öner/istockphoto.
com, 3 ©Fernando Alonso Herrero/istockphoto.com, 4 ©Image Source/Getty
images; p. 7 ©Chris Schmidt/istockphoto.com; p. 18 r ©Raido Väljamaa/
istockphoto.com, l ©leungchopan/istockphoto.com; p. 42 ©Muharrem Öner/
istockphoto.com; p. 44 1 ©Nicholas Monu/istockphoto.com, 2 ©e_rasmus/
istockphoto.com, 3 ©Huchen Lu/istockphoto.com, 4 ©bobbieo/istockphoto.
com; p. 60 l ©Justin Horrocks/istockphoto.com, r ©Phil Date/istockphoto.
com; p. 61 ©Leah-Anne Thompson/istockphoto.com; p. 62 ©flyfloor/
istockphoto.com; p. 63 ©drbimages/istockphoto.com; p. 67 ©drbimages;
p. 85 ©Fernando Alonso Herrero/istockphoto.com; p. 86 a ©Bartosz
Hadyniak/istockphoto.com, b ©Alan Tobey/istockphoto.com, c ©v0v/
istockphoto.com, d ©orkneypics/Alamy, e ©Cindy Hopkins/Alamy; p. 93
t ©The Power of Forever Photography/istockphoto.com, c ©Nabi Lukic/
istockphoto.com, b ©Cliff Parnell/istockphoto.com; p. 94 ©itanistock/
Alamy; p. 119 ©Elena Elisseeva/istockphoto.com; p. 129 4 ©Getty images;
p. 164 tl ©Jan Rysavy/istockphoto.com, bl ©Steve Froebe/istockphoto.com.
tr ©Chris Elwell/istockphoto.com, cr ©Claudia Dewald/istockphoto.com, br
©malerapaso/istockphoto.com; p. 165 l ©Claes Torstensson/istockphoto.com

Author acknowledgements

The authoring team would like to thank Clare Sheridan, Ian Morrison, Nick
Robinson, Nik White, Vanessa Manhire, Chris Capper and Ian Collier for
their constant help and support. We also offer our grateful acknowledgement
to Sarah Clark, Fred Gooch, and Neil McSweeney for their advice and
contributions to the manuscript. Finally, we would also like to thank all ELT
and academic skills staff and students across Kaplan International Colleges
for their assistance in trialling the materials during development and for their
valuable feedback and suggestions.

Publisher acknowledgements

The authors and publishers would like to thank the following people
who reviewed and commented on the material at various stages: Michael
McCarthy, Jenifer Spencer, Dr Mike Courtney and Debbie Goldblatt.

Design and illustrations by Hart McLeod, Cambridge

Skills for study Contents

Map of the book

	Part A Understanding spoken information	Part B Understanding written information
1 Approaches to learning 	Understanding types of listening Using note-taking techniques Understanding strategies for effective listening Understanding the purpose of lectures Following lectures effectively	Recognizing types of academic text Choosing appropriate reading strategies Using skimming, scanning and intensive reading Taking notes while reading
▶ UNIT TASK Approaches to learning		
2 Communication 	Preparing for listening by predicting content Listening actively Taking effective notes while listening	Assessing the usefulness of texts Identifying key points in texts Reading actively Analyzing texts
▶ UNIT TASK Modern media		
3 Science and technology in society 	Understanding signposting in lectures Identifying restatement Predicting content from language cues	Reflecting on challenges in academic reading Reading for a purpose Reading for detailed information Using sources to support your ideas
▶ UNIT TASK Packaging and waste		
4 Health issues	Understanding different types of signposting Understanding the speaker's purpose Understanding the speaker's attitude to the information	Understanding ways to improve your reading Reading to compare information Writing effective summaries
▶ UNIT TASK Health expectancy		

Review
Good study practice checklists
Appendices

Part C Investigating	Part D Reporting in speech	Part E Reporting in writing
Understanding more about learning methods in higher education Finding source materials Understanding source references Using library catalogues	Participating in tutorials Generating and organizing ideas Reflecting on your discussion skills	Understanding different types of academic writing Using a process approach to academic writing Understanding essay questions Developing a thesis statement Using sources in your writing
Understanding the benefits of group work Planning for successful group work Understanding different roles in a group Understanding and dealing with problems in group work	Sharing tips for giving presentations Identifying good presentation techniques Planning a presentation Opening a presentation Planning and practising an introduction Using visual support Concluding a presentation	Understanding plagiarism Paraphrasing text Summarizing text Using quotations
Evaluating sources Evaluating a range of texts Using sources effectively Using headings and subheadings to locate information Using contents pages to locate information Using index pages to locate information	Understanding what makes a good presentation Organizing a presentation according to its purpose Using visual aids in a presentation Designing appropriate visual aids	Creating thesis statements Identifying different essay structures Developing a topic sentence Developing ideas in writing
Keeping detailed records Recording correct bibliographic information Keeping a detailed scientific logbook Establishing the relevance of abstracts Identifying common features of abstracts Using an abstract for research	Defining a purpose for a presentation Being aware of your audience Giving effective pair presentations Planning and producing a poster	Writing an introduction Writing a conclusion Reviewing your written work

Introduction
Good study practice

Before you start to use this book, complete the questionnaire. Decide whether each statement is true (T) or false (F) for you. Then work in pairs and compare your approaches to learning. Come back to the fourth column when you have finished studying the entire book, and consider if any of your opinions have changed.

	You	Your partner	After you complete this book
1 I like to participate actively in class discussions.			
2 I like to review what I've learned in class and think about how it's connected to other things I know.			
3 I think it's important to listen carefully to the tutor and remember everything in lectures.			
4 I like to develop my understanding of a subject by doing extra research by myself.			
5 I think studying is enjoyable because it's interesting.			
6 The main purpose of studying is because it's useful for a future career.			
7 If I have a question about my courses, I like to get the answer from my tutor first.			
8 If I have a question about my courses, I try to search for the answer in my coursebooks.			
9 I think it's important to memorize the information that my tutor gives me.			
10 I think it's important to give original opinions in class and in my writing.			
11 I focus on preparing well to pass my exams.			
12 I want to study to broaden my understanding of a subject because it will help me in real life.			
13 I think it's important to consider new ideas critically to decide whether I agree with them or not.			
14 I think it is important to accept the ideas that the tutor tells me.			

Unit 1   Approaches to learning

Unit overview

Part	This part will help you to …	By improving your ability to …
A	**Be an effective listener**	• understand types of listening • use note-taking techniques • understand strategies for effective listening • understand the purpose of lectures • follow lectures effectively.
B	**Understand and compare academic texts**	• recognize types of academic text • choose appropriate reading strategies • use skimming, scanning and intensive reading • take notes while reading.
C	**Research and describe academic texts**	• understand more about learning methods in higher education • find source materials • understand source references • use library catalogues.
D	**Participate in academic discussions**	• participate in tutorials • generate and organize ideas • reflect on your discussion skills.
E	**Write an academic essay**	• understand different types of academic writing • use a process approach to academic writing • understand essay questions • develop a thesis statement • use sources in your writing.

Understanding spoken information

By the end of Part A you will be able to:

- understand types of listening
- use note-taking techniques
- understand strategies for effective listening
- understand the purpose of lectures
- follow lectures effectively.

1 Types of listening

1a Work in pairs. Look at the situations below where students need to listen to English at college or university. Match the situations (1–5) with their possible purposes (a–e).

Situation

1	Lecture
2	Class or tutorial/seminar
3	Presentation
4	Discussion with classmates
5	Talking with friends

Purpose

a To give students an opportunity to speak at length on a topic they have researched

b To discuss projects and study arrangements

c To provide students with information or ideas relating to a course of study

d To socialize

e To allow detailed discussion of ideas presented in a lecture

1b Think of at least three other situations at college or university where you may need to listen to English. Write them below.

Other situations
1
2
3

1c Listening to lectures can sometimes be difficult. Work in pairs. Write down three things you might do to make the situation less difficult.

Making listening to lectures less difficult
1
2
3

1d Work in groups and compare your suggestions.

2 Using note-taking techniques

> Taking notes is an important part of listening to lectures. Good note-taking requires practice. Throughout this course, you will be given lots of opportunities to develop your note-taking skills.

2a Match the sentence beginnings (1–7) with the sentence endings (a–g) to reveal some advice on effective note-taking.

1 Don't write down everything ...	**a**	short.
2 Keep your notes ...	**b**	your notes and add any extra points.
3 Don't write full ...	**c**	and well organized.
4 Make sure your notes are tidy ...	**d**	for long words and drawing simple diagrams to represent ideas.
5 After the lecture, review ...	**e**	explanations and detailed descriptions.
6 Review your notes ...	**f**	regularly.
7 Try using abbreviations ...	**g**	that you hear.

2b Check your answers with a partner and add some more suggestions of your own for effective note-taking.

Suggestions for effective note-taking

3 Effective listening

> To be an effective listener, you need to engage with what the speaker is saying and make sure that you hear and understand as much as possible.

1.1

3a Listen to a short talk given by a tutor to a group of students during their induction week on the topic of 'listening for study'. Write notes about any suggestions the tutor makes.

Before listening	While listening

3b Compare your notes with a partner. What might you have done before or during *this* listening task to make your listening more effective?

3c Look at the table below and tick (✓) which three strategies would be most helpful to you. Add any other strategies you can think of.

	You	Your partner
1 Be clear what the topic of the class or lecture is before it begins.		
2 Prepare carefully before the class or lecture by reading what is required.		
3 When you pre-read, make notes or leave space to add any interesting points that you hear in the class or lecture.		
4 Try to predict some of the topics and key topic vocabulary you are likely to hear during the lecture or discussion.		
5 Ask questions about ideas that are not clear – either during the lecture or at the end.		
6 Any other suggested strategies (give details)		

3d Work in pairs. Ask your partner which three strategies they think are most useful.

3e Tell the class which three strategies your partner prefers and why.

4 Understanding the purpose of lectures

4a Work in pairs. Discuss these questions and make brief notes of your ideas. Leave additional space – you will be adding to them later.

1 Are lectures an effective way of teaching? Why / why not?

2 Why are lectures so commonly used in higher education teaching?

3 Why should you attend lectures?

4b Read this extract from an article on lectures and make any necessary additions or changes to your notes from 4a.

Lectures

Whatever subject you choose to study, lectures are almost certain to be an important part of your student life.

We take it for granted that lecturing is a natural feature of higher education, even though we have probably all experienced difficulty in understanding lectures, or even staying awake through some of them! In fact, we have known for over forty years now that lectures are not the most effective way of teaching or learning. In 1968, the educational sociologist Lancelot MacManaway studied two groups of students. One group was asked to listen to his lectures and take notes, and the other group were not made to listen to the lectures themselves, but simply given a paper script of everything he would have said in the lecture and asked to read it. He found that the students who read the script actually got more benefit from it, and showed a greater level of understanding, than those who had listened to his lectures. But if lectures are not an ideal teaching method, why do we still use them? What is the real purpose of lectures, and how can we make sure that we get the most out of them?

The word *lecture* itself comes from the Latin word meaning 'to read'. The term has been around since the fourteenth century, and tells us a lot about how we think about education. Lectures in their earliest form developed as a way of spreading information at a time when books themselves were relatively rare and precious items, and access to libraries and the information they contained was severely restricted. So lectures, literally readings from key books to an interested audience, became a way of transmitting knowledge. The lecturer or tutor possessing knowledge which they pass to their students (who presumably are believed to have none) remains to this day a common understanding of the process of education, and perhaps explains why lectures are still so widely used. A 1994 study by Geoff Isaacs found that most academic staff share common ideas about the purpose of lectures. Out of 100 academics interviewed by Isaacs, around three quarters said that the purpose of lectures was to transmit important information from tutor to student, to provide a framework for the important ideas on a subject, to help students identify key points on a topic. This is interesting, because it suggests that lecturers are not speaking in the hope that you will understand everything. In fact, it seems that they are expecting just the opposite – that you will not understand everything. Therefore, the lecture is not intended as a complete guide to the topic, but an overview – a framework of key points, that the student can then go away and use to guide them in their own study later.

References

Isaacs, G. (1994). Lecturing practices and note-taking purposes. *Studies in Higher Education*, *19*(2), pp.203–216.

MacManaway, L. (1968). Using lecture scripts. *Higher Education Quarterly*, *22*(3), pp.327–336.

MacManaway, L. (1970). Teaching methods in HE – innovation and research. *Higher Education Quarterly*, *24*(3), pp.321–329.

4c Listen to a tutor giving a talk to students after they had read this article. Add to or change the notes you made on lectures in 4a.

1.2

5 Following lectures effectively

> The development of 'effective listening' is a key focus of this course and important to your achievements as a student.

5a Work in pairs. Decide whether each statement about effective listening is true (T) or false (F).

1 Effective listening includes understanding 100% of what the lecturer says.

2 Effective listening includes understanding the gist of what the lecturer says.

3 Effective listening includes the ability to predict what you will hear.

4 Effective listening includes writing useful notes quickly.

5 Effective listening includes thinking about how ideas are connected together as you listen.

6 Effective listening means you can remember what the lecturer said.

7 Effective listening includes asking the lecturer to be allowed to record their talk.

8 Effective listening means being able to understand different accents.

1.3

5b Listen to three people talking about what they think 'effective listening' is. Complete these notes about their main ideas.

Speaker 1: Student from non-English-speaking country
Take a note of …
Ask questions about …
Don't be …

Speaker 2: University lecturer
Don't try to understand …
Taking notes is important because …
Don't just try to …
Ask if it's OK to …
Think about …

Speaker 3: University lecturer
Take steps to make sure …
Read …
Try to predict …
Don't write everything …
After the lecture, …

> **UNIT TASK**   **Approaches to learning**

As you study each unit of this book, you will be asked to work on different stages of a task related to the theme or topic of the unit.

The Unit 1 task is about approaches to learning. At the end of each part, you will be asked to complete a stage of the task as follows:

Part A: Listen to an introduction on the topic.

Part B: Read two texts about it.

Part C: Do some further research for relevant material.

Part D: Have a group discussion on the topic.

Part E: Write an essay with this title:

Discuss how different approaches to learning can affect student success in higher education.

You are going to listen to a talk on deep and surface approaches to learning.

a   Work in pairs. Discuss what you think the terms *deep* and *surface* approaches to learning may mean. Make notes on your ideas.

1.4

b   Listen to a student advisor explaining what is meant by deep and surface approaches to learning. Check your answers to a.

c   Work in pairs. Look back at the questionnaire you did on p.6. Some of the sentences describe a surface approach and others a deep approach to learning. Discuss which ones might be called deep and which ones surface. Give reasons for your ideas.

Surface approach to learning	Deep approach to learning

d   Listen again. Add to or change your notes on deep and surface approaches to learning.

e   Work in pairs. Use your notes to discuss the differences between deep and surface approaches to learning and how you might adapt your own approach to be more successful.

Go to the checklist on p.175 and read the tips relating to Unit 1 Part A.

Understanding written information

By the end of Part B you will be able to:

- recognize types of academic text
- choose appropriate reading strategies
- use skimming, scanning and intensive reading
- take notes while reading.

1 Types of academic text

1a Work in pairs. Discuss these questions.

1 Do you read in your spare time? What kind of things do you enjoy reading?

2 Which of these texts do you expect to read most frequently during your studies? Can you think of any more examples?

magazine articles	newspaper articles	academic journals
emails	websites	textbooks
essays	lab reports	reports

1b Look at **Appendices 1**, **2** and **3** at the back of the book. Which of the above are they examples of? How do you know?

1c Read the texts in the Appendices quickly and complete the table.

		Text 1	Text 2	Text 3
a	What type of text is it?			
b	Who is the intended reader?			
c	What is the purpose of the text?			
d	What register is used (e.g. formal, informal, scientific, business, academic, etc.) (more than one register may be possible)?			
e	What different features does the text have (e.g. subheadings, diagrams, citations, etc.)?			

1d Check your answers in groups.

2 Choosing appropriate reading strategies

2a Work in pairs. Look at the different text types shown below and answer these questions. Give reasons for your answers.

1 Which texts would you read more/less carefully?

2 Which texts are likely to be more/less difficult to read?

3 Which texts might you make notes on? Why?

an email from your college/university

an email from your tutor giving feedback on your work

a chapter in a textbook

a magazine article

an email from a friend

2b Read the two texts from magazine articles and answer the questions below.

1 What is the best title for this article?

a Learning Cantonese

b Learning English

c Learning a new language

At any moment of any day, a huge number of people from almost every country in the world will be studying a new language. The reasons for studying may vary. Sometimes the reason is simply one of interest, sometimes it is because the student intends to visit a country that uses that language, and sometimes it is to help with a future career. Sometimes it is simply because the language is a compulsory subject at school or college. Whatever the reason, one thing that all language learners are certain to discover is that mastering a new language can be an extremely frustrating experience – and one which almost always leads the learner into embarrassing situations at some time or another. Just last week I took a taxi to visit my friend and decided to try out a few words I had recently learned in Cantonese. I leaned forward, tapped the taxi driver on his shoulder and said what I thought were the words for 'Block 4', the address of my colleague. The taxi driver looked very confused, and then started laughing. I later discovered I had confused the tones of the words for *Block 4* and had told him that he was dead!

2 Which languages are mentioned in this article?

Facebook Swahili version launched

More than 110 million speakers of Swahili will now be able to use the social-networking website, Facebook. The new version of the site has been launched by a group of Swahili scholars after receiving permission from the Californian internet firm.

Over the past five years, the use of Facebook has steadily spread in East and Central Africa, where most Swahili speakers live. Most experts predict that a Hausa version of the site could also be available soon in West Africa and a Zulu version for South Africa. The site already exists in South Africa in Afrikaans.

According to Symon Wanda, one of the project's organizers, a major reason for launching the Swahili site was to safeguard the future of the language. He said that the site was likely to be used mainly by younger people and by making a Swahili version available it would encourage the next generation to continue to use their native language. Mr Wanda argued that, 'They can easily navigate through when it's in a language they understand, which makes it easier to use Swahili than to use English.'

Sources in Nairobi say that the Swahili site has already been on trial for some time and word has spread quickly.

2c Work in pairs. Discuss how you approached the reading task above by answering these questions.

1 Did you read each text word by word?
2 Did you read the whole text and then go back to look for the answers to the questions or did you read the text focusing only on the questions?
3 Was your approach to the two texts the same or different? If different, why?
4 Which task did you find easier? Why?

2d Give a summary of your approaches to the class.

3 Skimming, scanning and intensive reading

In 2b above you were asked to read in two different ways. First, you were asked to decide what the best title for the article was. This required you to *skim* the text to get a general understanding. Then you were asked to find specific information on languages. This required you to *scan* the text for relevant information. Whether you find a relevant text by skimming or specific information by scanning, you might then need to read the selected text *intensively* (i.e. more carefully and with fuller understanding).

3a Practise skimming and scanning texts. Follow these instructions.

  1 Skim read the texts in **Appendices 1**, **2** and **3** and identify which contain information on different approaches to learning.

  2 Scan the texts and underline information about how the culture of the learner and learning institution affects students' approaches to learning.

> Choosing the right way to read something is a good reading strategy that will save you a lot of time. A good reader will choose to read different things in different ways, depending on what kind of information they are looking for.

3b How would you read the following? Would you skim, scan or read the text intensively – or a combination of these?

  1 Reading a letter from your college or university to find what dates your exams are.

  2 Reading an article on the economy in SE Asia to get a general idea of the writer's ideas on the topic.

  3 Reading a lab report to find out what measurements you need for your experiment.

  4 Reading a text to discover the writer's stance towards a topic.

  5 Reading the first paragraph of a text to decide whether it is relevant to your project.

  6 Reading the Table of Contents of a book to find chapters likely to contain relevant topics for further reading.

  7 Reading the discussion section of a lab report to see how well the results have been interpreted.

  8 Deciding which link to click on in a web search.

  9 Reading an article to find the percentage of people affected by global warming – and then to discover exactly how they are being affected.

3c Check your answers with a partner.

3d You are studying tourism at university and have been asked by your tutor to gather information on why the numbers of visitors to London are steadily declining and what suggestions have been made of ways to reverse this trend.

Look at the Appendices and, using scanning and intensive reading, find any information in the text which is relevant to the task and make brief notes.

Reasons for the decline in visitors	Suggested solutions

4 Taking notes while reading

> Reading is an active process and many people find it helpful to take notes. There are different approaches to note-taking and one method may work well for some people but not for others. You need to develop your own methods of taking notes. Efficient and effective note-taking will save you time and improve the quality of your work.

4a Work in small groups. Describe how you take notes when reading and then discuss which of the methods in your group seems the most effective.

4b Look at these two methods for taking notes. Which do you think is the most effective? Why?

I like to be really detailed with my notes. When I'm reading, I use my highlighter to highlight anything that I think is important, then I copy out the highlighted sections into my notebook. I then check all the vocabulary and write translations next to anything I'm not sure about. This way I make sure I don't miss anything important and I can understand everything when I read my notes again later.

Su-Bin, 23, Korea

First I read the article quickly to see if there's anything important and then I underline the key bits. Then I write the notes in my notebook. I use a lot of abbreviations and I use my highlighter and use arrows to connect ideas. I also like to make notes of questions I have on anything in the article if something is not clear to me. I always make sure I write the name of the article and the author too.

Abiola, 18, Nigeria

4c Read these statements. Tick (✓) the ones you agree with.

1 Notes should be arranged to help you organize your thoughts.

2 Everybody writes notes in the same way.

3 You should use your own words as much as possible in your notes.

4 You don't need to make a note of the page number.

5 You should explain difficult vocabulary in English rather than write translations.

6 You should use symbols to show connections between ideas.

7 Effective note-taking uses simplified grammar.

8 You shouldn't include your own ideas.

9 You should avoid abbreviations because no one will be able to understand what you've written.

10 You must include details of where you get the information from.

11 You should make a note of headings and subheadings.

4d Discuss your answers in groups.

4e You have been asked to prepare for a class discussion on problems associated with examinations. Check the Appendices for any relevant texts and write notes on the topic.

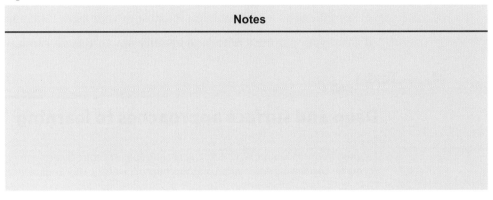

Notes

4f Work in groups of three. Read each other's notes and, using your answers from 4c, give suggestions as to how the notes might be improved.

4g Work in groups of three. Use your notes in 4e to discuss some of the problems associated with examinations. Do not refer back to the text in the Appendices. Each person in the group should summarize the information on one of questions 1–3 below. Then, as a group, discuss question 4.

1 How does a 'surface approach' make exam results meaningless?

2 What problems can exam stress cause?

3 Do exams encourage good teaching?

4 What kind of student performs better in academic contexts?

4h Summarize your group's ideas on question 4 for the rest of the class.

> **UNIT TASK** **Approaches to learning**

In this unit task, you will research information on this essay title:

Discuss how different approaches to learning can affect student success in higher education.

a Work in pairs. Underline key words in the essay title. Discuss which information from the unit task listening in Part A is relevant to the title.

b Skim read the two texts below on the topic of deep and surface approaches to learning and make notes on:

- information about the difference between deep and surface approaches to learning
- author(s)
- who the text is aimed at
- what the purpose of the original article was.

c Scan the texts for information relevant to your essay. Make notes.

d Read your partner's notes and identify any further research which is needed.

Text 1

Deep and surface approaches to learning

Source:
Adapted from: Houghton, W. (2004). *Engineering Subject Centre Guide: Learning and Teaching Theory for Engineering Academics.* Loughborough University: HEA Engineering Subject Centre.

Introduction

In this document we look at the concept of approaches to learning. The original study into this issue was carried out by Marton and Säljö (1976) and explored students' approaches to learning a particular task. Students were given an academic text to read and were told that they would subsequently be asked questions on that text. The students adopted two different approaches to learning, one of which can be called *deep*, and the other, *surface*.

Deep and surface approaches

The idea that students can, and do, take a deep or surface approach to their learning is probably one of the most used pieces of educational research in higher education, especially in engineering.

Simply stated, deep learning involves the critical analysis of new ideas, linking them to already known concepts and principles, and leads to understanding and long-term retention of ideas so that they can be used for problem solving in unfamiliar contexts. Deep learning promotes understanding and application for life. In contrast, surface learning is more superficial acceptance of information and memorization as isolated and unlinked facts. It leads to short-term retention of material for examinations and does not promote understanding or long-term retention of knowledge and information.

Critical to our understanding of this principle is that we should not identify the student with a fixed approach to learning, but it is the design of learning opportunity that encourages students to adopt a particular approach. We need to analyze the way we are teaching and identify the most likely methodology to encourage deep learning.

Designing for deep learning

Very crudely: deep learning is the best approach, better than surface learning, and teachers should teach in a way that encourages students to adopt a deep approach, although achieving this is not so easy.

Perhaps the strongest influence on students' approaches to learning is assessment. It is often argued that the setting of 'straightforward' assessments involving short questions testing separate ideas will encourage surface learning. However, this is not necessarily the case as even the most apparently simple assessment questions can ask students to demonstrate that their knowledge can be applied, which requires a deep approach to learning.

Basic principles and approaches to learning

The evaluation of process is very valuable in determining the depth of learning, but if we concentrate on process alone, we risk losing sight of the structure of the material being learned. Engineering, like mathematics and science, is a hierarchical subject. Working with the laws of Kirchhoff, Thévenin, Norton, for example, will lead to a deeper understanding of earlier principles, but learning cannot start there. Attempting to work with more complex principles without a good grasp of the more basic principles from which they are built can only lead to frustration and a surface learning approach in which students attempt to memorize solutions to complex problems they cannot understand. Encouraging students to practise the application of simpler principles will not force them to adopt a deep approach to learning, but it at least makes it possible.

Teachers need to think carefully and analytically about the assessment and assessment processes, as it is this part of the curriculum that affects students' approaches to learning most. Teachers need to construct assessment that gives students the opportunity to receive feedback, but also must make the assessment relevant to the real world of engineering.

References

Marton, F. & Säljö, R. (1976). On qualitative differences in learning – 1: outcome and process. *British Journal of Educational Psychology*, *46*, 4–11.

Text 2

An introduction to approaches to learning

Source: Fenton, R. (2012). *Strategic Study*. London: Marsh.

Introduction

Current educational philosophy tends to view the student as being more important than the teacher, especially with regard to independent study. Some tutors demand far more of the learner than they did in the past. This may be due to an expectation among academic staff that students will always be highly motivated by interest in their own subject areas. The very definition of what it means to be a student in many cases rests on this expectation. Barnett, for instance, defines a student as 'someone who … throws herself into her studies' (Barnett, 2007, p.18). Courses and assessments are frequently designed on the assumption of deep student interest and desire for knowledge.

With the increased focus on the centrality of students in the learning process, particular attention has been paid to the way that students approach their studies. The concept of deep and surface approaches to learning, first suggested by Marton and Säljö (1976), has had a profound influence on teaching theory. The consensus among academic staff is that deep approaches are superior to surface approaches, and it is these which they would expect their students to adopt. It is widely acknowledged that more effective teaching is that which can help students to develop a deep approach, while less effective teaching methods concentrate on rote learning and exam performance, resulting in a tendency for students to adopt surface approaches. Thus, while the engagement and actions of the learner remain central to the learning process, it is believed that better teaching creates a natural demand for deep learning in students.

A surface approach to learning

Students who take a surface approach to learning tend to be those who see education solely as something necessary for career success. Consequently, they have less interest in their subject matter, and value the tangible outcomes of their studies – satisfactory grades, passing exams, and gaining certification – more than the growth of knowledge itself. Students who take a surface approach study only what they are required to do in order to successfully complete their courses, and in this way are more passive learners than those taking a deep approach. Learners taking a surface approach are less likely to spend time doing extra research in order to fully understand a subject. Such learners also take a narrower view of their subjects than deep learners do. The knowledge they gain in one area tends to stay there; they tend not to make connections between ideas in different subject areas. In this sense, surface learners are more reliant on their teachers: they expect to be told, essentially, what they should be learning, and believe that if they diligently study what the teacher has assigned to them, then they will be successful in their assessments. As a consequence, surface learners depend more heavily on rote memorization of details provided in lectures or course books, and they are less successful at applying the knowledge they gain in their studies to new areas.

A deep approach to learning

Students who take a deep approach, on the other hand, are more active learners. They tend to be more interested in their subjects, and are more motivated by curiosity and a desire to learn than by the promise of high grades or success in exams – they feel a 'need-to-know' (Biggs, 1999, p.16). For a deep learner, the subject itself has intrinsic value. They study more dynamically than surface learners, spending extra time to fully understand the subjects that they learn, and, if necessary, reading beyond what their teachers have assigned to them. They have a clearer understanding of the connections between ideas and information. Where a surface learner is motivated primarily by the hope of success (or at least by fear of failure), a deep learner's main motivation is the hope of understanding. Deep learners are more intellectually curious than those taking a surface approach; indeed Laurillard (1993, pp.53–54) argues that the curiosity of a deep approach to learning may be necessary for success in higher education, as the complexity of many academic texts makes true understanding of their meanings impossible if one does not engage actively with the material. Deep learners, motivated by a desire for meaning, are better able to do this than surface learners, who tend to focus only on key words, phrases and ideas.

Research shows clear differences in the defining characteristics of student approaches to learning. However, it would be a mistake to characterize any student as taking a deep or surface approach all the time. Instead, it is more likely that students tend to adopt different approaches in different contexts. A simple distinction, therefore, between deep and surface learners is not necessarily an accurate picture of student learning styles. The most successful students are likely to be those who take a blended approach, and combine the positive aspects of surface approaches (memorization when necessary, and goal focus) with the interest and engagement in a subject that is typical of the deep approach.

References

Barnett, R. (2007). *A will to learn: being a student in an age of uncertainty.* Maidenhead: Society for Research into Higher Education and Open University Press.

Biggs, J. (1999). *Teaching for quality learning at university.* Buckingham: Society for Research into Higher Education and Open University Press.

Laurillard, D. (1993). *Rethinking university teaching, a framework for the effective use of educational technology.* London: Routledge.

Marton, F. & Säljö, R. (1976). On qualitative differences in learning – 1: outcome and process. *British Journal of Educational Psychology, 46*, 4–11.

 Go to the checklist on p.175. Look again at the tips relating to Unit 1 Part A and tick (✓) those you have used in your studies. Read the tips relating to Unit 1 Part B.

Investigating

By the end of Part C you will be able to:

- understand more about the learning methods in higher education
- find source materials
- understand source references
- use library catalogues.

1 Types of learning

1a Work in pairs. Label the diagram below with learning methods used in higher education.

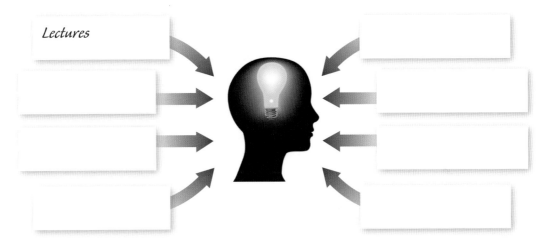

Lectures

1b Look again at your suggestions above and discuss which methods you are familiar with and which ones are new to you. Rank them (1–8) in order of familiarity.

> Students are often most familiar with learning methods which involve a tutor giving them information to learn. However, in your college or university studies much greater responsibility for your learning is passed to you – you will be expected to use strategies for learning independently, and this will often involve doing research. This could be for the purpose of writing an essay or report or simply to build on your knowledge of a topic. Eventually you may have to do an original piece of research for a longer project or thesis. Depending on which type of
> degree you are doing, you are likely to be involved in the following three types of research:
> - tutor-/lecturer-guided research
> - individual secondary research
> - individual primary research.

1c Work in pairs. Discuss what you think each type of research may involve.

1d Read the descriptions of types of research (a–c) and match them with the terms (1–3).

1 Tutor- or lecturer-guided research

a Where the student is doing some kind of research project on their own and searches for and finds texts and information by themselves. The student does not collect raw data directly but uses data published by other researchers. Using the resources of a library allows the student to collect data on a large scale and reach general conclusions. It also allows students to find out gaps in knowledge which may form the basis for new enquiry.

2 Individual secondary research

b Used when a topic has not been studied before. The student carries out a new investigation to produce original results through fieldwork, direct observation or experiment. The student is responsible for collecting new raw data by themselves.

3 Individual primary research

c The student is introduced to a topic and encouraged to learn more by their tutor, who may provide a reading list of both key and supplementary texts for the student to investigate, or guide them through a controlled laboratory experiment.

1e Work in pairs. Discuss the advantages and disadvantages of each type of research. Write notes in the table.

	Advantages	Disadvantages
Tutor-guided research		
Individual secondary research		
Individual primary research		

1f Work in pairs. Discuss which of the three types of research outlined above is most likely to be done in these contexts. Why?

1 a taught first-year module

2 a research project

3 a third-year dissertation

1g Find out what modules you are likely to take in the course you have chosen to study. You could look at the college or university website or prospectus or talk to a staff member from that department. In which modules are you likely to be expected to do your own research? Is it more likely to be primary or secondary research?

2 Finding source materials

It is common, especially in your first year of study, for your tutor to give you a reading list containing recommended texts – sources of information which can be used to help you develop your understanding of a subject. The list will often be written in reference form, containing important information to help you identify and find the source materials.

2a Work in pairs. Match the source types (1–4) with the references (a–g).

1 A book

2 A chapter, written by one author and appearing in a book edited by another

3 A journal article

4 An article on a website

a Alderson, J.C. (2000). *Assessing Reading*. Cambridge: Cambridge University Press.

b Alderson, J.C. & Buck, G. (1993). Standards in testing: a survey of the practice of UK examination boards in EFL testing. *Language Testing*, *10*(2), 1–26.

c Chapelle, C. (1998). Construct definition and validity inquiry in SLA research. In Bachman, L.F. & Cohen, A.D. (Eds.), *Interfaces between Second Language Acquisition and Language Testing Research* (pp.32–70). Cambridge: Cambridge University Press.

d Council of Europe. (2001). *Common European Framework of Reference for Languages: Learning, Teaching and Assessment*. Cambridge: Cambridge University Press. Retrieved January 30, 2009, from: http://www.coe.int/t/dg4/linguistic/cadre_en.asp

e ELGazette. (2007). *The main exams in English language testing*. Retrieved July 2, 2009, from: http://www.elgazette.com/language_testing.cfm

f Gardner, H. (1991, December). Do babies sing a universal song? *Psychology Today*, 70–76.

g Rey, G. (2000, August 11). Going Native. *The Times Online*. Retrieved July 2, 2009, from: http://www.timesonline.co.uk/tol/incokingFeeds/article767872.ece

A *journal* is an academic magazine which contains information about the latest research in an academic field. Scholars submit *articles* to the journal, giving details about their research. A single *issue* of a journal is like a single issue of a magazine; it contains several articles, as well as book reviews, comments, and other news. All of the issues for a particular period are collected into something like a large book called a *volume*; for example, in 2001 the Harvard Law Review published its 114th volume, containing the eight issues of that journal published during the previous year.

Traditionally, students were able to visit the library to look at a particular article in a volume of a journal, just like a chapter in an edited book. These days, however, many journal articles are available online. Most library websites have a separate portal or gateway for searching for electronic journal articles.

2b Work in pairs. Discuss these questions about the references in 2a. Write notes in the table.

1   What do the dates in brackets in each reference refer to?
2   Why do references d, e and g have two dates included? What is the difference between the two dates?
3   In reference c, what does (pp.32–70) refer to?
4   In reference b, what does *10*(2), 1–26 refer to?
5   Why do references d and e not provide an author name?

	Notes
1	
2	
3	
4	
5	

2c Compare your answers with the rest of the class.

> Just because a text is on the list it does not mean that you have to read it. Your tutor will probably tell you which items on the reading list are the most important.

3   Understanding source references

> Reading lists provided by your tutor generally use the same format as the reference section given at the end of essays, articles or reports to indicate what sources were used in the writing of the work. References contain all the information you need to find a particular source. There are many different ways in which this information can be written and most college and university departments have their own preferred style. Harvard style is one common referencing system and is used for the references given in this course.
>
> There are different ways of referencing for different kinds of sources; however, most referencing styles will include whichever of the following details applies to a particular source:
>
> - Last name of **author**(s)
> - **Initials** of author(s)
> - Name of **editor**(s)
> - **Publication date**
> - **Title** of book
> - **Title** of article
> - Internet **retrieval date**
>
> - **Edition number** (of journal)
> - **Volume number**
> - **Page numbers** of article (within the journal)
> - Where it was published (**location**)
> - Name of **publisher**
> - Name of **journal/magazine/newspaper**
> - **URL** (if an internet source)

3a Work in pairs. Annotate each part of the references below with the appropriate word from the information box on p.26.

Example

Author	Initials	Publication date	Title	Journal	Page numbers
Burns,	R.M.	(1995, January).	Data analysis for accountants.	*Financial Review, 23*	12–13.

1 Prosser, M. & Trigwell, K. (1998). *Teaching for learning in higher education.*

   Buckingham: Open University Press.

2 Marton, F. & Säljö, R. (1976). On qualitative differences in learning – 1:

   outcome and process. *British Journal of Educational Psychology, 46,* 4–11.

3 Gross, P. (Ed.). (1987). *A dictionary of economics* (6th ed., Vol. 1).

   London: Sirius Press.

4 Lublin, J. (2006). *Deep and surface approaches to learning: an introduction.*

   Birmingham: The Higher Education Academy C-SAP. Retrieved July 23rd, 2009,

   from: http://www.c-sap.bham.ac.uk/resources/guides/student_learning.htm

3b What type of source does each reference in 3a come from (e.g. a book, a journal article)?

4 Using library catalogues

Almost all libraries have online catalogues. These allow students to search for the materials they want in various ways. If you know the title and the name of the author, it is easy to find the material you want. But if you are searching for material on a specific subject, you may have to try using a number of different search terms.

For example, if you want information about **oil production in America**, you might try varying your search terms in the following ways:

1   Use synonyms.
    • America – USA/US
    • production – output

2   Use general words or expressions to widen your search.
    • oil production – oil industry
    • oil – fossil fuels/hydrocarbons/energy
    • America – global/worldwide

3   Use different combinations of key words.
    • USA oil production
    • US oil industry
    • America fossil fuel production
    • USA oil industry output

4a Work in pairs. Look at these topics. Brainstorm synonyms and general expressions that you could use to vary your search terms.

Topic	Synonyms	General expressions
Rainforest destruction in the Amazon		
The uses of artificial intelligence in business		
Challenges in modern hotel management		

When searching on topics, you may find a lot of sources which look useful because the title is similar to the topic you are researching. However, not all of these sources will actually be connected closely enough to the topic you want. When you find possible sources, skim read them to decide if they are relevant. Be critical and reject any that seem unsuitable.

4b You are an engineering student looking for books on study skills. You enter *study skills* as a subject in the online catalogue and this is the list of results. Work in pairs. Discuss which books you would choose and why.

	Author	Title	Ed./Year	Location	Holdings
1	Finch, Emily and Fafinski, Stefan	Legal Skills	2nd ed. 2009	Main Library	Availability
2	Johnson, Stuart and Scott, Jon	Study and Communication skills for the biosciences	2009	Science Library	Availability
3	Burns, Tom and Sinfield, Sandra	Essential study skills: The complete guide to success at university	2nd ed. 2008	Main Library	Availability
4	Cottrell, Stella	The study skills handbook	3rd ed. 2008	Main Library	Availability
5	Whitehead, Elizabeth and Mason, Tom	Study skills for nurses	2nd ed. 2008	Medical Library	Availability
6	Pritchard, Alan	Studying and learning at university: vital skills for success in your degree	2008	Main Library	Availability

On online library catalogues you may come across the following links:

Full details
If you click on this, you will get more information about the item, including the number of pages and a summary of the contents.

Location
Many large universities have more than one library. This tells you which one the item is kept in.

Holdings
If you click on *availability*, it will tell you how many copies the library holds and if they are available to borrow or out on loan.

Approaches to learning

In this unit task, you will continue to research information for this essay title:

Discuss how different approaches to learning can affect student success in higher education.

To help you develop your ideas, you are going to research the topic of the essay title by using the Internet and your university or college library.

a   Write a list of the keywords from the title that would form the basis of your search terms.

b   Now think of possible synonyms for each of the key words you have identified.

c   Use your answers to a and b to make a list of five possible search terms. Make a note of each term.

Possible search terms
1
2
3
4
5

d   Compare your suggestions with a partner. Which terms do you think would be the most successful? Why?

e   Before the next lesson, complete these tasks:

1   Search for reading sources using the five search terms from c.

2   Prepare a reading list of the sources you found useful to share with other members of your class. Use Harvard style for referencing.

3   Read and take notes on some of the most relevant sources on your reading list.

Go to the checklist on p.175. Look again at the tips relating to Unit 1 Parts A–B and tick (✓) those you have used in your studies. Read the tips relating to Unit 1 Part C.

Reporting in speech

By the end of Part D you will be able to:

- participate in tutorials
- generate and organize ideas
- reflect on your discussion skills.

1 Participating in tutorials

1a Work in pairs. Discuss these questions and write your ideas in the second column of the table.

	Your ideas from discussion	Ideas from Audio 1.5
1 Why are tutorials important?		
2 What are you expected to do in tutorials?		
3 In what ways might you benefit from tutorials?		

1.5

1b Listen to two students in a tutorial discussing the questions in 1a and write their ideas in the third column of the table. Compare their ideas with yours and identify any differences.

1c Listen again and answer these questions.

1 Did both speakers contribute to the discussion equally?

2 In what ways could either speaker have contributed more to the discussion?

3 What might both speakers have done to improve communication?

1d Check your answers with a partner.

1e What problems do you have in discussions? Say which are true (T) for you.

1 I am worried that my English is not good enough.

2 Other people won't let me speak.

3 I don't want to stop other people if they have good ideas.

4 Everybody else seems to have better ideas than me and know more about the topic than I do.

5 I am concentrating so much on what I want to say and how to say it that I lose track of the discussion.

6 In my culture, it is rude to argue with somebody if you disagree with them.

7 I just find it difficult to get into the discussion – I have ideas, but can't find a way to express them to the rest of the group.

8 I feel a little bit embarrassed giving my ideas because I am not confident in the subject.

9 I am shy and I feel uncomfortable talking in a group.

1f Work in small groups. Discuss how you might overcome each of the problems in 1e.

1g Share your suggestions with the rest of the class.

2 Generating and organizing ideas

2a Work in small groups. Your tutor has asked you to prepare for a tutorial discussion on *ways of organizing ideas*. Read this article, which outlines one approach to generating and organizing ideas. Have you used this approach?

One of the most innovative thinkers on the topic of creative writing is Tony Buzan. In his book *Use Your Head*, he describes a process he calls a *mind map*. This has become popular among tutors and professionals of various kinds and has been given many different names, such as *brain map* or *spider map*. Mind mapping begins by writing down any central idea which provides the main focus of the activity – for example, *entertainment* or *agriculture*, or even something more abstract such as *hope* or *revenge*. This is written in the middle of a blank page, and a circle is drawn around the word.

Circles containing related ideas are then jotted down around the word; these are joined to the main word using lines. This is where the title *spider map* or *spider diagram* comes from, because the diagram soon begins to look like a spider's body, with the main idea in the middle and lines stretching outwards from it like a spider's legs. Ideas connected with these related ideas are then added where appropriate so that in the end a whole structure of related ideas can be seen on a single page.

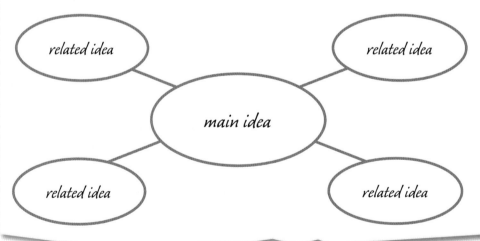

2b Work in small groups. Discuss what you think about this approach for generating and organizing ideas.

2c Look at these tips for generating and organizing ideas for a discussion. Do you do any of these things when preparing for and participating in discussions?

1 Read some information about the subject and make clear and effective notes.

2 Make a list of questions to discuss.

3 Think about the topic before the discussion and make notes of your ideas.

4 Participate fully and make valuable contributions.

5 Share your ideas.

Brainstorming is a well-known method of using writing to generate and organize initial ideas on a topic. When you brainstorm, you think about a particular topic or question and then write down everything and anything that comes to mind while you think about it. When you brainstorm, you shouldn't worry too much about spelling, grammar, punctuation, or even whether your ideas seem 'correct' or not. It is important only to get ideas down on paper quickly; after that you can review what you have written and decide what is useful or not.

2d Work in pairs. Look at some different ways to write ideas while brainstorming. Answer these questions.

1 What topic do the three brainstorms deal with?

2 What are the differences between the three brainstorming methods?

3 Which method do you prefer? Why?

A **Simple brainstorm**

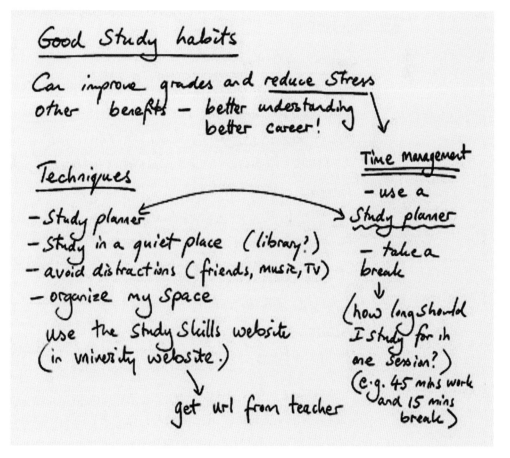

B Bullet point list

Good Study habits

Benefits
- Deep understanding
- Better grades
- Less stress

Time management
- Study planner
- fixed times
- Include breaks

Resources
- 'Study Skills' book
- University website

Techniques
- Quiet place
- Avoid distractions
- Organize space
- Organize folders

C Free-writing

Good Study habits.

Good Study habits can help improve understanding and also grades and reduce stress — better time management is key to this — e.g. work with a Study planner, do work in advance, take regular breaks etc.

techniques for good study? → Work in library or a quiet place, avoid distractions like music etc. Carry a folder — organize work Space and folder.

lots of Study skills resources to help improve study habits — many books in the library on this subject, also check university websites for advice.

2e Work in pairs. Discuss the advantages and disadvantages of each method. Share your ideas with the rest of the class.

2f Work in small groups. Use one of the suggested brainstorming techniques to develop ideas on the following topics:

1 The importance of examinations to learning

2 The differences between studying abroad and at home

3 The role of education in a country's development

4 Higher education's role in preparing students for life

5 Advantages and disadvantages of university entry requirements

3 Reflecting on your discussion skills

3a Work in new groups. Choose one of the topics that you brainstormed in 2f. Hold a short discussion on the topic.

3b After the discussion, work in pairs. Discuss how well you feel the discussion went. What could you do next time to improve your participation in the discussion?

> **UNIT TASK** **Approaches to learning**

In this unit task, you will prepare and take part in a group discussion on this essay topic:

Discuss how different approaches to learning can affect student success in higher education.

During the discussion, you will need to discuss

- the approaches to learning you have learned about
- the advantages and disadvantages of each approach
- how the approaches may be more or less suitable for different students (personalities, ages, levels of education, cultural backgrounds, etc.)
- which approach your group believes to be the most effective for student success in higher education.

a Before the discussion, review your notes and re-read relevant articles. Use a suitable technique to organize your ideas.

b Work in small groups and discuss the topic.

c Complete the self-appraisal form below.

	1	2	3	4	5	
I made clear and effective notes on the relevant articles.						My notes were difficult to understand.
I made a list of questions on the articles.						I didn't think of any questions.
I thought about the topic before the discussion and made notes of my ideas.						I did not think about the topic much before we started the discussion.
I participated fully and meaningfully and made valuable contributions.						I didn't say anything at all.
I shared ideas and cooperated fully with other students in a sensitive way.						I didn't listen to other students.
I made clear and effective notes during the discussion.						My notes were unclear and ineffective.
I am very satisfied with my overall participation in the discussion.						I am not at all satisfied with my overall participation in the discussion.

 Go to the checklist on p.175. Look again at the tips relating to Unit 1 Parts A–C and tick (✓) those you have used in your studies. Read the tips relating to Unit 1 Part D on p.176.

Reporting in writing

By the end of Part E you will be able to:

- understand different types of academic writing
- use a process approach to academic writing
- understand essay questions
- develop a thesis statement
- use sources in your writing.

1 Types of academic writing

1a What do you think you will be expected to write at college or university? Match the text types (1–8) with the definitions (a–h).

Text type		Definition
1	Notes	**a** An informal description of a scientific experiment taken during the experiment
2	Report	
3	Lab report	**b** A written record of the main points of a lecture or a text for the student's personal use
4	Log book	**c** A detailed examination of a particular process or situation over time
5	Essay	
6	Thesis/dissertation	**d** A timed piece of writing on a topic discussed in lectures and tutorials
7	Exam answer	**e** A long piece of original research usually done at an advanced level of study
8	Case study	

f A formal piece of writing to describe an experiment and discuss ideas relating to the results of the experiment

g An objective piece of writing reflecting facts or results of a survey or research

h A formal piece of writing used to make an argument or discuss a statement

1b Which of these types of writing would you only use in science subjects? Which do you think will be most commonly used in your own discipline?

2 Using a process approach to academic writing

The process approach to writing essays allows time for self- and peer-checking of early drafts of your work. Revisions are then incorporated into a final draft or submission. Adopting a process approach will improve your written work.

1.6

2a Listen to the first part of a lecture in which a teacher explains the process approach. Write notes under heading 1 (The 'visionary' stage).

> **Notes on the process approach to essay writing**
>
> **1** The 'visionary' stage (planning)
>
>   **a**
>
>   **b**
>
>   **c**
>
>   **d**
>
> Take a break!
>
> **2** The 'revisionary' stage (evaluating and revising)
>
>   **a** Content editing
>
>   **b** Structural editing
>
>   **c** Copy editing (or proof-reading)

1.7

2b Now listen to the second part of the tutor's explanation. Write notes under heading 2 above (The 'revisionary' stage).

3 Understanding essay questions

As you heard in 2a, the first stage of the process of writing an essay is understanding exactly what the question is asking you to do. When you get an essay title, you might begin by asking yourself four questions.

1   What is the precise meaning of all of the main terms used in the title?

Example
Approaches to learning vary from culture to culture and institution to institution. Discuss.

You may need to consider and define the precise meaning of *approaches to learning, culture* and *institution*.

2   What are the assumptions behind the title?

Example
Examine the ways in which different approaches to learning affect rates of examination success.

This title assumes that approaches to learning affect examination success. So you should not be arguing whether or not this is true.

3   What do the instruction words in the title mean?

Example
A title using *Discuss* will be very different from one using *Examine* (see 3b below for more information)

4   How many parts are there to the title, and therefore to the essay?

Example
Approaches to learning vary from culture to culture and institution to institution. Discuss.

This title has at least two distinct parts: an essay would consider first how approaches to learning vary between cultures, and second how they vary between institutions.

3a Work in pairs. Look at the sample essay questions a–c. Discuss these questions.

1 Which words would you need to consider carefully and clearly define before you can write your essay?

2 Are any assumptions being made in each title?

   a A deep approach to learning is more effective than a surface approach. Discuss.

   b IT developments have resulted in great improvements in education. Discuss.

   c How have changes in teaching styles over the past 50 years affected the quality of university and college graduates?

3b Here are some common instruction words used in essay titles (1–10). Match them with the definitions (a–j). Add two more instruction words and their definitions to the table.

Directive word		Definition
1 examine	**a**	to look for similarities and/or differences between two or more things
2 describe	**b**	to give the main facts about something
3 discuss	**c**	to give a good reason for something
4 analyze	**d**	to study something in detail, in order to discover more about it
5 compare	**e**	to consider something in order to make changes to it, give an opinion on it or study it
6 explain	**f**	to look at or consider a topic carefully and in detail, especially by separating it into its parts, in order to understand or explain it
7 justify		
8 review	**g**	to make something clear by giving information about it
9 summarize	**h**	to write about different opinions on a subject in detail; to present different viewpoints on the topic and give your own conclusions about them
10 outline		
	i	to express the most important facts or ideas about something or someone in a short and clear form
	j	to say or write what something is like
11	**k**	
12	**l**	

3c Work in pairs. Discuss how many parts there are to these titles.

1 Describe the characteristics and uses of sodium chloride.

2 Compare and contrast teaching and learning styles in Chinese and British universities.

3 Analyze how religion, age and socio-economic levels are determining factors influencing attitudes towards women at work.

3d Discuss how you can apply the four questions we looked at on p.37 to your unit task title:

Discuss how different approaches to learning can affect student success in higher education.

4 Developing a thesis statement

In most academic essays, once you have analyzed the title, you need to develop a central thesis statement. The thesis statement contains an idea or belief about the topic that will be discussed in more detail in your essay. The thesis statement is usually one sentence in the introduction that makes a claim of some kind (for example: *The growing use of the Internet in universities has led to an increase in plagiarism*). In your essay, you need to present enough evidence in support of your thesis statement to enable you to draw conclusions at the end.

You can start thinking about the thesis statement by asking yourself these questions about the main concerns of the research:

1 Who will the essay focus attention on?
2 Where will the essay focus its attention?
3 How are the subjects of the essay being affected?
4 Why are the subjects being affected?
5 What is the relationship between the subjects?
6 When (i.e. what period of time) is the essay interested in?

Then use your answers to the questions to form the thesis statement.

4a Work in pairs. Answer questions 1–6 above in relation to this essay question.

Discuss the impact that the Internet has on university students' study habits.

4b Work in pairs. Think of at least three different possible thesis statements for your unit task.

Discuss how different approaches to learning can affect student success in higher education.
Thesis statement 1
Thesis statement 2
Thesis statement 3

5 Using sources in your writing

5a Work in pairs. Discuss these questions.

1 Why do you think it is important to use other people's ideas to support your work?
2 Why is it important to reference your sources in your work?

5b Read the following article. Work in pairs. Discuss what the writer's main point is.

Learning styles and students' attitudes toward the use of technology in higher and adult education classes

Thomas D. Cox, University of Memphis

Introduction

Education today is faced with the challenge of adapting to an environment of ever-increasing technological advances. The challenge for educators is to utilize this technology in ways that facilitate the highest level of learning outcomes. The educational community has growing concerns about the effectiveness of technology such as CD-ROM, videotapes, multimedia presentation software, World Wide Web (WWW) discussion forums, and the Internet to meet the needs of students when utilized in the classroom (Lukow, 2002). Thus, it can be said that while technology use in the classroom is copious, improving learning through the application of this technology should remain the goal.

There are several issues that may arise when applying technology in the classroom. Among these are (a) choices about which technology to use (Bascelli, Johnson, Langhorst & Stanley, 2002), (b) how effective technologies are in reinforcing learning (Grasha, 1996), and (c) technology's role in shifting from an instruction paradigm, which is teacher focused, to a learning paradigm, which is student focused (Van Dusen, 1997).

Shifting the classroom perspective from teachers to students must involve recognizing learning styles of students. Subsequently, teachers must adjust teaching strategies to accommodate different styles. Given the amount of literature about how 'learning style' is actually defined, the following definition addresses the role of the individual in learning. Learning style can be defined as the general tendency towards a particular learning approach displayed by an individual (Keefe & Ferrell, 1990; Robotham, 1999). In other words, students may prefer one approach to learning over other approaches.

If the goal of educators is to increase learning outcomes, addressing the issues involved in using technology in the classroom and accommodating student learning styles must be examined. Although there are studies addressing the issues of technology integration into the curriculum and the attitudes of students toward the technology being used, there is limited research that links these attitudes to individual learning styles (Lukow, 2002).

Source: Cox, T. (2008). Learning Styles and Students' Attitudes Toward the Use of Technology in Higher and Adult Education Classes. *Institute for Learning Styles Journal*, 1, 1–13.

References

Bascelli, D., Johnson, K., Langhorst, R., & Stanley, T. (2002, April). *The connected classroom: Seeking appropriate technology choices in a small college campus and classroom*. Lecture conducted at the Seventh Annual Mid-South Instructional Technology Conference, Murfreesboro, Tennessee.

Grasha, A. (1996). *Teaching with style: A practical guide to enhancing learning by understanding teaching and learning styles*. Pittsburgh: Alliance Publishers.

Keefe, W., & Ferrell, B. (1990). Developing a defensible learning style paradigm. *Educational Leadership, 48*(2), 57–61.

Lukow, J. (2002). *Learning styles as predictors of student attitudes toward the use of technology in recreation courses*. Unpublished doctoral dissertation, Indiana University, Bloomington (UMI No. 3054366).

Robotham, D. (1999). *The application of learning style theory in higher education teaching*. Lecture presented at Wolverhampton Business School, University of Wolverhampton, United Kingdom.

Van Dusen, G. C. (1997). *The virtual campus: Technology and reform in Higher Education*. ASHE-ERIC Higher Education Report 25, No.5. Washington, D.C. The George Washington University, Graduate School of Education and Human Development.

5c Work in pairs. Read the article again. Discuss these questions.

1 Which ideas in the text are the writer's own? Underline these in blue.

2 Which ideas come from other sources? Underline these in red.

3 Why does the writer refer to other sources?

4 What kind of sources does the writer use?

5 How many sources does the writer give citation for?

6 Are all the cited sources mentioned in the list of references?

7 What information is given in the citations?

8 What information is given in the references?

9 What order are the references in?

> **UNIT TASK** **Approaches to learning**

Draw together all the work you have been doing in this unit on different approaches to learning. Write an essay of 400–500 words with this title:

Discuss how different approaches to learning can affect student success in higher education.

Remember:

• follow the suggestions made in Part E Section 2 'Using a process approach to academic writing'

• include a clear thesis statement

• use sources to support your ideas

• reference your sources.

 Go to the checklists on pp.175–16. Look again at the tips relating to Unit 1 Parts A–D and tick (✓) those you have used in your studies. Read the tips relating to Unit 1 Part E on p.176 and use them to help you improve your essay.

Unit overview

Part	This part will help you to …	By improving your ability to …
A	**Gain meaning from lectures**	• prepare for listening by predicting content • listen actively • take more effective notes while listening.
B	**Gain meaning and understanding from academic texts**	• assess the usefulness of texts • identify key points in texts • read actively • analyze texts.
C	**Work effectively in a group**	• understand the benefits of group work • plan for successful group work • understand different roles in a group • understand and deal with problems in group work.
D	**Deliver an academic presentation**	• share tips for giving presentations • identify good presentation techniques • plan a presentation • open a presentation • plan and practise an introduction • use visual support • conclude a presentation.
E	**Create a piece of academic writing**	• understand plagiarism • paraphrase text • summarize text • use quotations.

Understanding spoken information

By the end of Part A you will be able to:

- prepare for listening by predicting content
- listen actively
- take more effective notes while listening.

1 Predicting content

An important part of listening is using your knowledge of the situation and context to help you understand what is being said. For this reason, a student might read about a particular subject before attending a lecture on it, in order to provide some context for the lecture topic. Furthermore, experience of attending lectures will help the listener know what to expect in terms of style and structure. The listener might also be experienced at interpreting the lecturer's *body language*. Familiarity with the style and structure of a spoken genre also helps the listener. Most lectures, conversations, news reports, and many other kinds of spoken language are highly predictable due to the listeners' prior knowledge. Good listeners have some idea of what the speaker is going to talk about, what kind of words will be used and what direction the speaker will take. If a speaker doesn't follow a predictable pattern, it can be confusing, for example:

A   *What are you doing tomorrow?*
B   *Sally is sick.*

This short dialogue doesn't make sense because the answer is unexpected. However, if we know that Sally is B's daughter, we can use this knowledge to understand that the speaker means he is staying at home to take care of her.

Listeners instinctively use this background knowledge to help them understand what is being said.

1a What expectations do these listeners have of the following kinds of communication?

1   An audience at a sales presentation

   The audience will be expecting to hear more information about the product. They might expect the speaker to use a lot of persuasive, positive and descriptive language, to convince them to purchase the product. The speaker may appeal directly to them through the use of personal pronouns. It may be a short presentation, so that the audience doesn't lose interest.

2   A student listening to a lecture at university

3   Someone listening to a conversation between a customer and a clerk in a bank

4   Someone listening to an argument between a couple

5   A tutor listening to a classroom discussion

1b You are going to listen to part of a lecture about body language. Work in pairs. Look at the examples of body language in pictures 1–4 on p.44. Discuss how each student might be feeling and why.

1c Does everyone in the class interpret the body language in the pictures in the same way?

1d The part of the lecture you will hear focuses on the following two things:

1 a definition of 'body language'

2 the reasons why body language is important for communication.

Work in pairs. Discuss what you think the lecturer will talk about in each of the areas mentioned above.

2.1

1e Listen to the lecture. As you listen, write notes on the two parts of the lecture.

Body language
1 Definition
2 Why body language is important for communication

1f Were your predictions in 1d correct?

2 Listening actively

2a Look at the list of things that people might do while listening to a tutor or lecturer. Which things do you do while listening? Tick (✓) the items in the 'You' column.

	You	Your partner
1 I listen and take notes of anything I hear.		
2 I consider the speaker's point of view, and if I agree or disagree.		
3 I listen and take notes of key points.		
4 I listen to hear how much the speaker agrees or disagrees with the ideas they are describing.		
5 I compare what the speaker is saying with notes I made earlier while pre-reading about the topic.		
6 I make notes of things I want to ask questions about.		
7 I listen to hear if the tutor mentions any important writers on this topic, so I can research them later.		

> It is important to listen actively to a speaker in a class or lecture. You should adopt strategies such as making notes, considering whether you agree with the speaker's point of view, and thinking of questions to ask at the end of the lecture. These strategies can help you focus your attention and listen effectively.

2b Ask a partner what things they do while listening and find out why they do them. Tick (✓) the items in the 'Your partner' column.

2c Gestures and body language may mean different things in different cultures. What do the following mean in your culture?

1 Sticking your thumb up
2 Someone smiling at you
3 Kissing someone on both cheeks
4 Somebody bowing to you
5 Forming a 'V' shape with your fingers
6 Someone patting you on the head
7 Someone pointing at you with their index finger
8 Someone giving you something with one hand
9 Someone refusing to shake your hand
10 Giving someone a big hug

2d What is the difference between *gesture* and *body language*? Do you think that any of the gestures and body language in 2c mean the same thing in every country? Discuss your answers with the class.

2e You are going to listen to a short talk about how body language can cause misunderstandings between cultures. Before you listen, work in pairs and discuss these questions.

    1 Have you ever experienced a breakdown in communication or misunderstanding with someone from a different culture or country because of body language? What happened?

    2 Do you think that misunderstanding body language can have a serious effect on communication? Can you think of any specific examples of this?

2f Listen to the talk and take notes on the key points. Make a note of any questions you would like to ask.

2.2

2g Listen again. What is the speaker's general opinion of this subject? Do you agree or disagree with the speaker? Why?

3 Taking effective notes

3a Work in pairs. Look at the notes made by the two students below. Discuss which style you prefer.

Student A – Linear notes

Is body language the same everywhere?

thumbs up   shake of the head

smiles/frowns   shyness/disgust, fear, surprise

Student B – Mind map notes

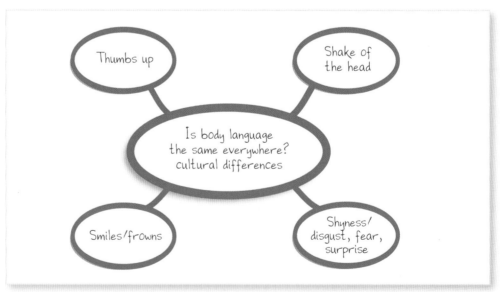

3b These notes are rather basic and will be of little use. Remember that you may need notes later for revision. Use your own notes from 2f to add more details to the notes above. Discuss and decide exactly where these details should be put. Could the examples above be arranged differently?

3c Look at the opinions about what makes effective notes below. Tick (✓) the ones you agree with.

1 Good notes use symbols and abbreviations to save time and space.

2 There is a special style of note-taking symbols and abbreviations which you must learn.

3 Good notes should be written in full sentences.

4 Good notes are well organized.

5 You should rewrite your notes to make them look nice.

6 You should use bullet points and subheadings to organize the information.

7 Good notes should be written in your own words.

3d Work in small groups. Discuss the reasons for your answers.

3e Work in pairs. Look at two students' notes about the lecture on body language. Using your answers from 3c, discuss the notes. What are the good and bad points of each set of notes?

Student A

Universal body language

· Overseas students can answer it — is it the same everywhere?

· Differences everywhere?

· Allan Pease's 1981 book called 'Body language' says that British and American 'thumbs up' is OK but in Greece it is rude.

· In Bulgaria, shaking the head means yes but in many other countries it means no.

· Smiles and frowns are understood everywhere

Human universals

· In a 1991 study, Donald Brown, an anthropologist at UC Berkeley said:

· Shyness expressions are universal

· Facial expressions for disgust, surprise, fear are the same

· But these things are not exactly the same everywhere — they are varied in different places.

· It's a good idea to be observant in a new country.

Universal body language
- Same everywhere??
- Allan Pease – 1981 'Body language'
   Brit and US 'thumbs up' = OK / Greece = rude.
    Bulgaria, shake head = yes but many other countries = no.
- Smiles and frown understood everywhere.
- 1991 Brown,

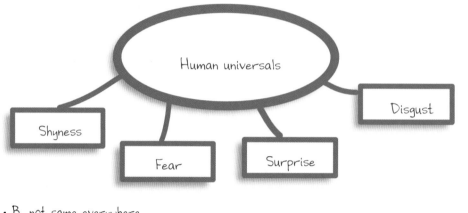

- B. not same everywhere
- Be observant – new country

3f Complete this table of common symbols and abbreviations.

≠	not the same as	§	section
±	neutral	~	about/approximately
>		∴	therefore
<		w/	with
=		min	
&		max	
→	leads to / causes	govt	
←	results from	c.	
↓	decrease	vs	
↑		ft	
/	per	yrs	
p	page	N.B.	
pp		cf.	compare
@		w/o	without
re		%	

3g Check your answers with a partner.

3h Look again at the abbreviations for 'feet' and 'years'. How have these words been abbreviated?

> There are other ways to write notes faster and help yourself to listen more effectively.
>
> • Don't write words like *a, an* or *the*.
>
> • Abbreviate by only writing the first syllable or two of longer words, e.g. *estimate – est, democracy – democ, problem – prob.*
>
> • To describe a process taking place you would normally write *-ing*, e.g. *increasing.* This can be shortened by simply adding *g*, so *falling* would become *fallg*, or even ↓*g*.

3i Work in pairs. Take turns reading the sentences aloud and writing brief notes.

1 Government spending on education fell last year.

2 Gas prices are rising by about seven per cent each year.

3 The meaning of the thumbs up symbol is not the same in Greece as it is in the United States.

4 The average male needs between 2,000 and 2,500 calories per day. Consuming much more or less than this can lead to a range of health problems.

5 We will not be able to understand it fully without more research.

6 For homework, look at Section 13 in your textbooks, as well as the special report on pages 22 and 23.

3j You are going to hear part of a lecture on how birdsong is affected by early conditions in the nest. Consider these questions to help you predict what the lecturer will discuss.

1 Why do birds sing?

2 How can the health of the bird affect their song?

2.3

3k Listen and take notes on the key points.

Birdsong
Reason(s) birds sing
Research
Birds that were healthier in the nest
1
2

3l Check your answers with a partner.

3m Work in pairs. Discuss these questions.

1   Can you understand your notes when you read them again?

2   Have you used symbols and abbreviations to make your notes shorter? If not, why did you choose not to?

3   Have you written in your own words? If not, why did you choose not to?

4   What could you do next time to improve your notes?

> **UNIT TASK**   **Modern media**

The Unit 2 task is about how media such as the mobile phone and the Internet are changing the way people use their leisure time. At the end of each part, you will be asked to complete a stage of the task as follows:

Part A: Listen to an introduction on the topic.

Part B: Read two texts about it.

Part C: Do some further research for relevant material.

Part D: Give a short presentation on the topic.

Part E: Write an essay with this title:

What are the most important sources of news for young people today?

a   Work in pairs. Discuss what is meant by the term *modern media*. What methods do you use to communicate with friends and family?

b   You are going to listen to a media analyst explaining the latest research on changing patterns of media use. Work in small groups. Discuss what you expect to hear in this talk. Write notes.

Changing patterns of media use

c   Listen to the talk and add to your notes above. Organize your notes so that they will be useful to you at a later date.

2.4

d   Work in small groups. Discuss whether the predictions you made in b were helpful. Why / why not?

Go to the checklist on p.177 and read the tips relating to Unit 2 Part A.

Understanding written information

By the end of Part B you will be able to:

- assess the usefulness of texts
- identify key points in texts
- read actively
- analyze texts.

1 Assessing texts

> If you are using material which is not on your reading list, you need to consider whether a source is reliable. Texts which are useful in academic work should be *accurate*, *objective* and *up-to-date*.

1a Match these expressions to their definitions.

1 Accurate	a The writing considers all points of view on the subject, even ones which contrast with the writer's own.
2 Objective	b The work has been written recently, or the information it contains is still relevant.
3 Up-to-date	c The information in the text is precise, and the facts are correct.

> *Audience*, *purpose* and *text source* also influence the content of texts. When you are reading, ask yourself these questions:
> • Why was this article written? To inform? To persuade? To explain?
> • Who is the intended readership? Local? International? Experts? Non-specialists?
> • What is the writer trying to achieve?
> • Where does the text come from?

1b You are researching communication for a class discussion. Your tutor has asked you to discuss this topic:

Discuss how the Internet facilitates communication.

Read the following texts and assess how useful each one might be for your discussion using the three questions above. Complete the table.

Text	Useful? (yes/no)	Reasons
A		
B		
C		
D		

A

How do Europeans use the Internet in their daily lives?

Since 2000, the Bamford Institute has conducted an annual study about the Internet activities of the average European. This report provides a summary of the key findings from the 2005 study. Details on the survey methodology used in the study are available in appendix C. Below is a list of the main findings of the study, with elaboration provided in the next section.

Johnson, T., Stoyanova, R. & McKee, S. (2005). *How do Europeans use the Internet in their daily lives?* Bamford: Bamford Institute of Sociology.

B

The death of the press

A hundred years ago, news was exclusively provided by newspapers. There was no other way of supplying the latest information on politics, crime, finance or sport to the millions of people who bought and read newspapers, sometimes twice a day. Today the situation is very different. The same news is also available on television, radio and the Internet, and because of the nature of these media, can be more up-to-date than in print. For young people, especially, the Internet has become the natural source of news and comment.

This development means that in many countries newspaper circulation is falling, and a loss of readers also means a fall in advertising, which is the main income for most papers. Consequently, in both Britain and the USA newspapers are closing every week. But when a local newspaper goes out of business, an important part of the community is lost. It allows debate on local issues, as well as providing a noticeboard for events such as weddings and social groups.

All newspapers are concerned by these developments, and many have tried to find methods of increasing their sales. One approach is to focus on magazine-type articles rather than news; another is to give free gifts such as DVDs, while others have developed their own websites to provide continuous news coverage. However, as so much is now freely available online to anyone with a web browser, none of these have had a significant impact on the steady decline of paid-for newspapers.

Sinharay, R. (2010, February 15)
The death of the press?
The Daily Times, pp.27–28.

C

Blogs, wikis and podcasts

Personal authoring technologies have made it easier than ever for instructors and students to contribute their thoughts, experiences, and opinions to a global discourse. In addition, these technologies provide a rich opportunity for instructors to focus their students' attention on discipline-specific questions related to a single course or topic.

This article provides details on blogs, wikis, and podcasts in order to critically assess their instructional value and creative potential, as well as the IT infrastructure required to support them. We will demonstrate the numerous technologies people are using; discuss the application and assessment of these technologies; present an overview of IT support challenges; and provide hands-on experiences with the production of blogs, wikis, and podcasts. The article will conclude with a discussion of other personal authoring technologies emerging on the educational horizon.

Jennings, P. (2007, January 15) Blogs, wikis and podcasts. *Education Blog.* Retrieved from http://www.blog.com/jenningsp

D

Trends in media use among young people

In 2007, a report (Newspaper Research Foundation, 2007) was published on how young people around the world use traditional and new media. The report was compiled using groups of 15- to 24-year-olds in ten countries, including Colombia, Japan, the Philippines, Lebanon, Serbia, Spain and Sweden. One of the main findings was that the young people regarded traditional media such as newspapers as more reliable and accurate than newer media such as the Internet. Despite this, many of the respondents said that 'discussion with friends' was their main source of news, and social networking sites were also regarded as an important channel of information.

It appears that although young people are aware that news from friends and family may not always be accurate, they prefer not to rely on one single source, instead collecting news from a variety of providers.

Another finding was that although the respondents used new media such as blogs and other internet sources, they still valued the traditional media formats, such as newspapers, more highly. However, they all said that new devices such as mobile phones and MP3 players were taking up time, which prevented them from reading newspapers as much as they would like. A related topic is the growth of free newspapers around the globe, especially those given to commuters on public transport in major cities. These are widely read by the young, and they claim that these free papers stimulate their curiosity about news and current affairs, driving them to read paid-for newspapers at home.

The findings of this report will be used to design further studies to explore the likely patterns of newspaper readership in the future.

Matthews, G. (2010, June 3). Trends in media use among young people. *The New Order*, pp.7–11.

2 Identifying key points in texts

When you have chosen an appropriate text, and you are sure that the text is reliable, you can read it for the information you need. As you read, look for the key points, to help you understand and remember what you are reading.

2a You are going to identify key points in short texts on the subject of the Internet. Work in pairs. Discuss these questions.

1 Is the Internet a reliable source of academic information? Why / why not?

2 What are the advantages of using the Internet for finding academic information?

2b Work in pairs. Read this text and choose the most appropriate title from 1–3. Discuss the reasons for your answer.

1 The Internet: its origins

2 The Internet: a global communication tool

3 The Internet: a limited information resource

The Internet is a worldwide network of information resources and is a powerful tool for communication. Information on virtually any subject may be found on the Internet and information servers are emerging globally. In the past, access to the Internet was mainly restricted to the academic community, but now the 'digital superhighway' is completely open for both business and home users.

The Internet offers people a powerful tool which may be used in a number of ways, including education, the collection and retrieval of information, and the rapid and automated distribution of information to large groups of people. In this article, the Internet and its facilities are considered, together with the resources available to people.

Adapted from D'Emanuele, A. (1995) The Internet: a global communication tool, *International Pharmacy Journal*, 9 (2), pp.68–72. Retrieved from http://www.pharmweb.net/pwmirror/pwf/pharmwebf1.html

In Unit 1 Part E you learned how to identify the central argument or *thesis statement*. The key points of a reading text tend to be those that support or add further information to the central argument.

2c Read the text in 2b again and underline the thesis statement. Then underline the information which relates to the central argument of the text.

2d Read the second part of the same text on p.55 and take notes on the points in the text which support the thesis statement.

Notes

The origins of the Internet can be traced to an information-sharing system developed by the US Department of Defence in the early 1970s (ARPA-Net). It has since grown into the present information-rich network of worldwide computer resources encompassing virtually every significant computer user in the world. Physically, the Internet is a worldwide interconnection of computer networks linking millions of computers – and millions of people.

The Internet should not be considered solely as an information resource, but also a powerful global communication tool. There are several ways in which people may communicate over the Internet and these will be described later. It should be borne in mind that whilst retrieving information or communicating using the Internet, a connection will not be direct to the remote computer, but via several other networks and computers (known as routers) that constitute the Internet. The actual route may even change during a communication. All this is invisible, however, and a connection appears as if a user is directly connected to the remote computer.

Adapted from: D'Emanuele, A. (1995) The Internet: a global communication tool, *International Pharmacy Journal*, 9 (2), pp.68–72. Retrieved from http://www.pharmweb.net/pwmirror/pwf/pharmwebf1.html

3 Reading actively

When you study an academic text, it is necessary to think about what you are reading. Reading actively may involve the following actions:

- evaluating other people's ideas
- finding support for your own ideas in other people's writing
- using other people's ideas to re-evaluate your own beliefs
- considering whether the writer is *subjective* or *objective* in his/her treatment of the subject.

3a What aspects of an academic text make it more subjective or objective? Write your ideas below.

Subjective	Objective

3b Compare your answers with a partner.

3c Look at these statements. Which are subjective and which are objective?

Statement	Subjective/ objective?	Reasons
1 Wikipedia is a free online information tool written collaboratively by volunteers from around the world.		
2 Wikipedia is an excellent tool for students.		
3 It cannot be relied upon since articles have not been peer reviewed and can be altered by anyone.		
4 Wikipedia cannot be regarded as a true encyclopaedia.		
5 It hosts over 2,000,000 articles on everything from Ancient Hebrew to Madonna.		
6 The editorial procedure ensures that content is reliable and relevant.		

3d Look at the statements you marked as subjective. Do you agree or disagree with these ideas? Give reasons for your opinions.

3e Work in pairs. Reread the texts in 2b and 2d. Are they subjective or objective? Discuss your ideas.

4 Analyzing texts

4a Work in pairs. Discuss these questions.

1 Do you use Wikipedia or any other online encyclopaedia?

2 What kind of information do you look for?

3 Do you think it is reliable?

4b Your tutor has asked you to discuss this topic:

Wikipedia cannot be regarded as a reliable encyclopaedia.

Work in small groups. With reference to Wikipedia, discuss the problems with using online encyclopaedias for research and suggest some possible solutions. Write notes below.

Notes

4c Read this extract from an essay written by a student on the same topic. Check whether any of your ideas from 4b are mentioned.

1 In recent times, there has been much debate about the influence of online resources such as Wikipedia in academic research. Wikipedia is considered to be a good research tool by some, while others doubt its credibility. Even though Wikipedia is a useful information resource, currently its suitability as an academic source is doubtful due to concerns over the accuracy of its information. However, by introducing expert review it is likely that this problem can be overcome. This essay will first outline some of the problems associated with Wikipedia and then examine some of the possible solutions that have been suggested for this problem.

2 Supporters of Wikipedia claim that the technological era has created access to information to all. Any contributor to Wikipedia may provide information in highly specialized fields. However, this strength is also arguably its greatest weakness. The fact that anyone can edit Wikipedia may make the contributions from experts less important. Individual contributors cannot be compared to an expert in a particular field merely by having access to information. For information to be considered reliable and authentic it must come from one who has spent much of their time on a particular topic, making him or her an authority in their field.

3 Moreover, even though Wikipedia is not an academic-level resource, it may be argued that the democratic nature of Wikipedia makes information unreliable. Even though the editing process of Wikipedia means misinformation is regularly corrected, it is impossible to remove bias and wrong information from all articles. This leaves Wikipedia open to criticism that its information is inaccurate and overly subjective.

4 There are a number of ways in which this problem could be resolved. Wikipedia itself now uses a system of registered administrators to monitor the quality of entries. In the light of recent scandals about the quality of these administrators, Wikipedia's operators are now much more cautious about ensuring their credentials. An alternative solution proposed from outside Wikipedia is the registration of qualified experts as reviewers. It may be argued that if Wikipedia is to be regarded as an academic source it must include some kind of expert review. These reviewers might be paid or contribute their expertise on an entirely voluntary basis. Supporters of this approach argue that the use of qualified and publicly acknowledged experts would be a simple and effective solution to the problem of credibility.

5 Though Wikipedia's attempts to improve the quality of its review procedures have undoubtedly helped to reduce the number of factual errors on the site, it is still not possible to guarantee the reliability of the content as long as a system of contribution by anonymous amateurs is used. However, expert review is also problematic. The review of content by expert administrators, whether paid or unpaid, would certainly improve the content authenticity of Wikipedia, allowing it to be more widely accepted by academics and educators. This is the method by which other encyclopaedias are created, and it is arguably true that Wikipedia will never be accepted as a suitable academic resource until it uses expert review of its content. However, there is a fundamental problem with this; introducing paid expert staff would undermine the basic idea of Wikipedia – that anyone with knowledge and interest can contribute, democratically and for the public good. Also, it is highly unlikely that sufficiently expert contributors and reviewers could be convinced to give their time to the project without payment.

4d Underline the thesis statement and key ideas in the text. Do you agree or disagree with them? Why?

4e Look at the text again. Match each paragraph (1–5) with its function (a–d).

Function	Paragraph	Notes from the text
a Give the background context (Situation)		
b Outline the issues (Problem)		
c Outline the responses to the issues (Response)		
d Evaluate these responses (Evaluation)		

4f Note down the main points of each 'phase' from the student's essay in the third column of the table.

> When you are reading academic texts for your essays or discussions, see if you can identify the argument structure. Use this as a framework to make notes.

➤ UNIT TASK **Modern media**

In this unit task, you will research information on this topic:

What are the most important sources of news for young people today?

a At this stage of your research, you should start to think about the unit task essay title in more detail and consider how best to start organizing your note-taking. At the end of Part C, you will be asked to find some additional sources of information on this topic yourselves, so you may want to consider which aspects of the essay title you need to find more information on.

b Read these two texts on young people and the media. Underline the main points and then take careful notes – you will need to use your notes in the next *Modern media* task.

Trends in media use among young people

In 2007, a report (Newspaper Research Foundation, 2007) was published on how young people around the world use traditional and new media. The report was compiled using groups of 15- to 24-year-olds in ten countries, including Colombia, Japan, the Philippines, Lebanon, Serbia, Spain and Sweden. One of the main findings was that the young people regarded traditional media such as newspapers as more reliable and accurate than newer media such as the Internet.

Despite this, many of the respondents said that 'discussion with friends' was their main source of news, and social networking sites were also regarded as an important channel of information.

It appears that although young people are aware that news from friends and family may not always be accurate, they prefer not to rely on one single source, instead collecting news from a variety of providers.

Another finding was that although the respondents used new media such as blogs and other internet sources, they still valued the traditional media formats, such as newspapers, more highly. However, they all said that new devices such as mobile phones and MP3 players were taking up time, which prevented them from reading newspapers as much as they would like. A related topic is the growth of free newspapers around the globe, especially those given to commuters on public transport in major cities. These are widely read by the young, and they claim that these free papers stimulate their curiosity about news and current affairs, driving them to read paid-for newspapers at home.

The findings of this report will be used to design further studies to explore the likely patterns of newspaper readership in the future.

Matthews, G. (2010, June 3). Trends in media use among young people. *The New Order*, pp.7–11.

How children use the media

Source: Lala, S., & Hall, J. (2010). Changing trends in childhood leisure. *Media Letters, 14* [(3), 207–211. (p.207).

A year-long study of media use by British children (6–17 years) has found that although they spend more time indoors using the Internet or watching TV than children in other countries, this is not always their choice. Their preference may be for outdoor activities, but for various reasons this may not be possible.

The study indicates that 99% of children watch television, on average for 2½ hours a day. Over 80% also watch DVDs and videos regularly. Computer games are also popular, with over two-thirds of children playing them. Nearly 90% also listen to music, but this is often while doing something else, such as homework. More than half read non-school books, with many reading an hour each day.

The reason why these activities are so popular seems to be that parents are worried about their safety outdoors, and that there is also a lack of places where children can go locally. This appears to be especially true of older children (over 11) who are less likely to attend organized leisure activities. It is interesting to compare this with the situation in other European countries; for example, only 34% of German and 21% of Swiss children complain that there is nothing to do locally, while in Britain the figure is 81% among 15-year-olds.

Significantly, when parents are asked about their concerns for their children, only 11% said that their neighbourhood was 'safe', although 56% thought that the streets where they had grown up were safe. The same parents listed fear of illegal drugs and crime as the main dangers their children faced. It appears, then, that these parents create media-rich home environments as a compensation for these perceived threats.

It was found that more than half the homes had cable or satellite television, thus providing children with channels offering dedicated programmes aimed at young people, such as cartoons. Large numbers of children were found to have their own personal stereo, TV and computer. Compared with other European countries, British children have far more screen media entertainment.

Despite this, the study suggests that given a choice, children prefer being outdoors with friends.Watching TV was widely considered as a second-best option, for when you were bored or tired. When asked to choose activities for an ideal day, 39% of children chose meeting friends and 35% playing sport, whereas watching television was only selected by 14%.

It appears, then, that although children in the UK have access to far more media than children in other countries, their use of this is partly a reflection of their parents' fears rather than their own choice.

Go to the checklist on p.177. Look again at the tips relating to Unit 2 Part A and tick (✓) those you have used in your studies. Read the tips relating to Unit 2 Part B.

Part **C**   Investigating

By the end of Part C you will be able to:

- understand the benefits of group work
- plan for successful group work
- understand different roles in a group
- understand and deal with problems in group work.

1   The benefits of group work

> Some students may be surprised to find they are expected to work in groups to complete certain academic assignments, e.g. preparing for seminar discussions. For those who have always worked on their own, this may cause some difficulties at first.

1a   Work in pairs. Discuss your experience of group work. What factors made it a good or bad experience?

1b   Work in pairs. Look at the opinions given about group work below. Discuss to what extent you agree or disagree with each person's opinion.

I hate working in groups.
It's always the same – one person takes over
and bosses everyone else around, or at least tries to.
And how can you be sure that everyone is going to make
as much effort as you are? It's frustrating if you're trying to
do your best but you know someone else isn't doing their bit.
That's particularly annoying if your group is getting a joint
mark for a project or something like that – it's like the
laziest people are getting a free ride.

Esther, 22, Nigeria

Working in
groups is not for me. I mean, I
know that you can get good results working
with others, but the problem is the pace of the work.
I really think it's a waste of time to have to keep meeting
to discuss things that you could do much faster by yourself.
Also, when you work alone, you know it's your own work and
you can take pride in that. Group work tends to mean that
everyone has to compromise so that good ideas may get
ignored just to keep group harmony.

Junxiang, 25, China

I quite like group work these days. I never used to see the point, but after doing it a few times, I know that the groups I've worked in have achieved things that were much better than any of us could have done alone. It's good to get fresh ideas, and really makes you realize how your own ideas are not always the best. It definitely isn't always easy to work in groups, because some people's personalities may clash and so on, but even that's good in the long run, because it's a kind of training for dealing with people in real life.

Mohammed, 26, Saudi Arabia

1c You are going to listen to part of a lecture on the value of group work. Before you listen, work in small groups and discuss the value of group work. Write your ideas below.

The value of group work

1d Listen and take notes on the main points of the talk.

2.5

1e Work in pairs. Discuss any differences between your opinions and experiences of group work and those mentioned by the speaker. Do you agree with the speaker? Why / why not?

2 Planning for successful group work

2a Work in pairs. Look at the list of suggestions for making your group work successful. Match the headings (1–7) with the paragraphs (a–g).

1 Analyze the task	**a** This is the most important test of your group's performance. When you have finished and handed in your work, it may be helpful to have a final meeting to discuss what you have all learned from the task.
2 Divide up the work fairly, according to the abilities of the members	**b** Someone needs to take notes about what was agreed at meetings and send these to all members as a reminder.
3 Make everyone feel included	**c** Get everyone to discuss the assignment and agree on the best methods to complete it. At this stage, it is important to have complete agreement on the objectives.
4 Finish the assignment on time	**d** Nobody should feel an outsider, so make special efforts if there is only one male student, or one non-native speaker, for instance. Make a list of all members' phone numbers and email addresses.
5 Get to know the other members	**e** Break down the task week by week and allocate specific roles to each member. Agree on times for regular meetings – although you may be able to avoid some meetings by using group emails. University campuses and libraries often have rooms that students can book to do project work together.
6 Select a co-ordinator	**f** Your group may include a computer expert or a design genius, so make sure that their talents are used for the benefit of the task. It is most important to make sure that everyone feels they have been given a fair share of the work.
7 Plan the job and the responsibilities	**g** Normally you cannot choose who you work with, so it is crucial to introduce yourselves before starting work. An informal meeting to get to know each other before you begin can help you work together more successfully.

2b Work in pairs. Add some more suggestions.

2c Work in pairs. Read these stories about unsuccessful group work. Discuss what Natalia and Leeming's groups could have done to work together more effectively.

We were supposed to be giving a short group PowerPoint presentation about what we'd learned at the end of our course. We didn't get off to a good start, really. We were all graduate students, so we thought we would all just be able to get along and work hard together without too much planning. We had a meeting at the beginning, and planned out roughly what we were going to do, but that took forever – everyone was arguing right from the start and no one listened to each other at all.

In the end it was a disaster. We nearly didn't finish it on time because the guy who was supposed to be making the slides had never used PowerPoint, and when he did finish, it was the morning of the presentation, so we didn't have a chance to practise together – not that the rest of them even seemed to care about practising.

Natalia, 20, Germany

We had to write a group report. We all got along OK in the beginning; in fact, maybe that was the start of the problem. We met a couple of times, in theory to talk it over, but mainly we just ended up getting to know each other and chatting. Anyway, after about three weeks we decided we needed to get on with it, and one of the guys in the group just turned into a complete control freak. He insisted that we needed a leader and that he should be in charge, and then started ordering us, basically, to do the jobs that he set for us. I think we were a bit lazy so we were glad to have someone in charge, and accepted his orders.

Leeming, 23, China

3 Understanding different roles in a group

Everyone has different ways in which they can contribute to a team. Knowing each other's strengths, weaknesses and preferences can help you to choose the right person for the different tasks that your group must carry out.

3a Meredith Belbin's 1993 book, *Team Roles at Work*, provides a useful guide to different roles that team members can play. Look at the list of roles identified by Belbin and complete the first two columns of the table on p.64.

- **Plant** – a creative person, who likes to contribute new ideas. They are not always very practical.

- **Resource Investigator** – someone who is good at finding and collecting information.

- **Co-ordinator** – the classic 'leader'; a more mature member of the group who helps to make sure that targets are set and achieved.

- **Shaper** – the kind of person who is good at asking challenging questions, who tests the ideas of the group and finds weaknesses in the work which need to be improved. They can occasionally cause offence by being too direct in their criticisms.

- **Monitor Evaluator** – someone who judges whether the work is being done well, and makes sure that the group is making steady progress. They sometimes lack drive and the ability to inspire others.

- **Teamworker** – someone who encourages a good group atmosphere. They are good at listening and averting friction.

- **Implementer** – a practical person who is good at taking responsibility and getting things done on time.

- **Completer Finisher** – a painstaking person, good at detailed tasks like spotting and fixing errors in the final product.

- **Specialist** – someone who can offer specific or rare skills to the group, for example using a particular software package, or subject-specific knowledge.

My usual roles in group work	My strengths in group work	My partner's strengths in group work

3b Compare your answers with a partner. Make notes in the third column of the table.

4 Dealing with problems in group work

Part of the challenge of working in groups is to learn how to manage any difficulties together.

4a Work in pairs. Brainstorm a list of problems that you might face while doing group work. Write notes below.

Potential problems encountered in group work

4b   Read about group problems 1–3. Are any of the problems you brainstormed in 4a mentioned?

1   In a group of six, you find that two students are not doing any work. Not only do they not come to meetings, they have not done the tasks they were given at the beginning. Should you …

    a   *decide that it is simplest for the rest of you to do the work of the missing students yourselves?*

    b   *find the students and explain that their behaviour is going to damage the chances of all six members?*

    c   *tell your lecturer about the problem?*

    d   *Alternative response:* _____

2   You are the only non-native speaker of English in the group. Although you can understand normal speech, the other students speak so fast and idiomatically that you have difficulty taking part in the discussions. Should you …

    a   *tell your lecturer about the problem?*

    b   *keep quiet and ask another student in the group to explain decisions later?*

    c   *explain your problem to the group and ask them to speak more slowly?*

    d   *Alternative response:* _____

3   One member of the group is very dominant. He/she attempts to control the group and is intolerant of the opinions of others. Should you …

    a   *explain to them, in a group meeting, that their behaviour is having a negative effect on the group's task?*

    b   *tell your lecturer about the problem?*

    c   *let them do all the work, because that's what they seem to want?*

    d   *Alternative response:* _____

4c   Work in small groups. For each of the group problems, add an alternative solution to the list in the space provided. Then decide as a group which solution you think is the best response.

4d   Read **Appendix 4**, which gives advice about how to work successfully as a group. Check your answers to 4c against the advice given. Make notes of any other tips that you think are useful.

> **UNIT TASK**   **Modern media**

In this unit task, you will continue to research information on this topic:

What are the most important sources of news for young people today?

You will also participate in a group discussion on this topic.

a   Work in small groups and read the task below. Use steps 1–4 in the checklist to plan your approach to the task.

Use the library and the Internet to find more information and research the topic. Try to make sure that you only use recent sources. You will need to paraphrase and summarize the information that you find. Remember to include references for the sources in your notes.

Checklist

1   Make sure that everyone understands the task.

2   Find out about each member's strong points – in what way will each person be able to contribute best?

3   Make a detailed plan – what do you have to achieve? How long will you need to do each task?

4   Divide up the work fairly between all members of the group.

b   Carry out the task. Then meet in your small groups to share your research findings.

c   As a group, discuss your favourite methods for getting news. You will first need to decide what you mean by 'news'. Decide if you think your experience in this area is typical of other people of your age. Keep a record of your discussion.

 Go to the checklist on p.177. Look again at the tips relating to Unit 2 Parts A–B and tick (✓) those you have used in your studies. Read the tips relating to Unit 2 Part C.

Reporting in speech

By the end of Part D you will be able to:

- share tips for giving presentations
- identify good presentation techniques
- plan a presentation
- open a presentation
- plan and practise an introduction
- use visual support
- conclude a presentation.

1 Sharing tips for giving presentations

1a Work in pairs. Discuss these questions.

1 Have you ever given a presentation?

2 How do you feel about giving presentations?

3 What did you feel confident about and what would you like to improve?

4 Think about a good or bad presentation you have seen. What factors made it good or bad?

1b Read the thoughts a student has on giving a presentation. Work in small groups. Discuss what difficulties Ricardo had, and how he coped with them.

When I was first asked to give a presentation at university, I had no idea what to do. I didn't really know the subject so I had to do a lot of extra reading. I made lots of notes and tried to include everything in my presentation. Before the big day, I practised in front of my friend, in front of the mirror; I even went to sleep dreaming of my presentation. When the day finally came, I was so nervous and it got worse because I had to wait ages for other people to finish. When it was my turn, I could hear my heart beat, but when I started talking I stopped feeling so nervous. The waiting was much more difficult than actually presenting. I was quite well prepared, but I talked for too long. One of the most difficult things for me was deciding what to leave out. But when I finished I felt pretty good and I gained confidence, not only in giving presentations, but in the knowledge of my subject too.

Ricardo, 23, Angola

1c In small groups, use your ideas from 1b to develop a set of seven tips for giving successful presentations. Include what to do and what **not** to do. Then add three more tips of your own.

Ten tips for successful presentations	
1	6
2	7
3	8
4	9
5	10

> At some time in your college or university studies, you will have to give an academic presentation. This is when you present a piece of research, a project or an essay, to an audience of fellow students or teaching staff. One thing you must remember is that *presenting* to an audience is definitely not the same as *reading* a piece of work *aloud*.

1d Work in pairs. Write notes on the differences between presenting and reading aloud.

Features of presenting	Features of reading aloud

2.6

1e Listen to two students giving a brief presentation on this topic and check whether you have thought of the same points. Modify or add to your notes if necessary.

2 Identifying good presentation techniques

2.7

2a Listen to a conversation on how to give a good presentation. As you listen, take notes under each heading in the table.

The speaker	Voice	Visual aids

2b Check your answers with a partner.

> In academic life, presentations are used to give the speaker the opportunity to explain a topic to a group of people with similar interests.
>
> Presentations are often used to assess students, so careful preparation and practice are necessary to keep the interest of the audience and avoid stress.

2c Make a note of the following.

1 Strong points in your presentation technique

2 Areas to improve

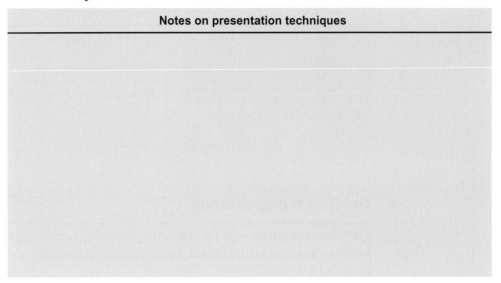

2d Discuss your answers with a partner.

3 Planning a presentation

Effective presentations need careful planning. Unless you organize your time carefully you may not be able to include everything you want to cover.

3a Look at this diagram of the structure of a presentation. Match the activities (a–j) with the stages of the presentation (1–4).

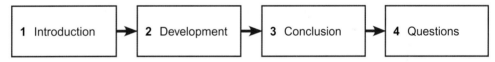

a Explain the background to the topic and what aspects you plan to talk about.

b Invite the audience to ask for more detail or clarification.

c Summarize your main points.

d Deal with each section of your talk in a logical manner.

e Give a simple outline of the presentation.

f Show visuals (graphs, maps or photos) to support your points.

g Suggest further possibilities for research.

h Provide examples where possible.

i Use signpost phrases (*the next issue …*) to help the audience follow the stages.

j Introduce yourself.

3b You have been asked to give a presentation on the discussion you had on Wikipedia in Unit 2 Part B, section 4. Work in pairs. What would you include in each stage of your presentation? Write a brief plan below.

Plan of Wikipedia presentation

4 Opening a presentation

Whether the audience is familiar with your topic or not, a good beginning to your presentation is important. Here are some commonly used strategies for making a good start:

- telling an anecdote
- referring to current affairs
- directly stating the topic of the presentation
- asking a rhetorical question
- asking a question to generate interest
- presenting a shocking or surprising fact
- using surprising statistical data
- sharing your personal experience
- citing a famous saying
- telling a joke.

2.8

4a Listen to the presentation beginnings and identify the strategy used in each presentation.

	Strategy
1	
2	
3	
4	
5	
6	

4b Work in pairs. Discuss which of the strategies in 4a would suit your preferred style of presentation. Have you used any of them? If so, were they successful?

4c Work in pairs. Plan how you might introduce a presentation on the topic of studying in a second language. Write brief notes below.

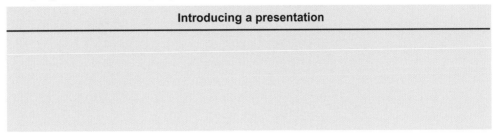

Introducing a presentation

2.9

4d Listen to a first-year student introducing a presentation on computer security. Answer these questions.

1 How does the student get the audience to focus on the topic?

2 How is the presentation organized?

5 Planning and practising an introduction

When presenting, it is a good idea to make notes on small cards, called cue cards, which can easily be held in your hand. This is the student's cue card for the introduction you heard in 4d.

> Presentation: Computer security
>
> 1
>
> Introduction (thanks, etc.)
>
> Any security problems for audience? – check
>
> – cyber attack: damage computers + steal personal data
>
> a) dangers, e.g. worms
>
> b) protection methods

5a Work on your own to prepare an introduction to the topic you planned in 4c. Your introduction should last for two minutes. Write notes on the main points on the cue card on p.72. Do not write out every word.

Introduction

5b Compare your plans with your partner from 4c. Discuss any differences and agree on the best version.

5c Work in groups of four. Take turns to give the introduction to your presentation. Then as a group, discuss how the introductions might be improved.

6 Using visual support

> When you are speaking to an audience, they are not just listening to your words, but also watching you. Your body language is part of the message. A speaker who wants to engage an audience must stand comfortably and use eye contact and gestures to support the talk.
>
> Similarly, if you only use words to explain your ideas, the audience has to listen very carefully. It is much better to help them by having some visual support, such as PowerPoint slides or a poster. In some cases, of course, real objects can also be used as an illustration.
>
> Slides are commonly used to show:
> - the title and subtitle
> - your name
> - an outline of the talk
> - the main points of different sections of the talk
> - statistical data
> - maps, charts and other graphics
> - photos and drawings.
>
> All of these can help the speaker present the information as clearly as possible. However, there are some potential dangers in using visuals.

6a Work in pairs and complete the table with possible advantages and disadvantages of using visuals in presentations.

Advantages	Disadvantages

6b Compare your notes with another pair.

7 Concluding a presentation

A presenter needs to signal to the audience that the presentation has nearly finished. Possible useful phrases here are:
- *So, to conclude this presentation, can I say …*
- *Finally, I'd like to point out …*

7a Can you think of any other expressions to indicate you are concluding your presentation?

Following one of these expressions, a presenter would usually summarize the main points of their presentation.

Some conclusions may then include a 'call to action' – in other words, a request from the presenter that the audience should consider doing something in response to what they have heard in the presentation. This may be a suggestion or a recommendation to the audience.

2.10

7b Listen to the conclusion of the talk on computer security. What was the 'call to action' the speaker made?

Most presenters finish by inviting questions from the audience. Getting a range of questions is a sign of a good presentation, since it means the audience are sufficiently interested to want to know more. However, it may seem difficult to have to answer them without preparation. One possibility is to write a list of possible questions before the presentation and think about how you would reply. You will probably find that you can give an answer to most. If you do not know the answer, say so, but indicate what you will do to find the answer, even if you say you will need to do some further research in that area. Nobody expects you to be the world expert on the subject! However, you could offer to contact them later, once you have found out the information they requested.

7c Work in pairs to prepare a conclusion for the topic you introduced in 5a. Then work with another pair and deliver your introduction and conclusion. Discuss with the other pair how the conclusions might be improved.

Modern media

In this unit task, you will prepare and give a presentation on this topic:

What are the most important sources of news for young people today?

a   Work in groups. Plan your presentation using the format Introduction – Development – Conclusion. Then divide up the sections between all the group members. The main section should include a summary of the research that you have read, as well as a summary of your own experience.

b   Prepare your part of the presentation, including designing some PowerPoint slides.

c   Practise the whole talk together in order to check that your timing is accurate.

d   Give your group presentation, and listen to other groups. As you listen to other groups give their presentations, you might want to take notes of anything you hadn't included in your own presentation.

Reflect on how well your team worked together by noting down your answers to these questions.

1   How well did your group foster a 'team spirit'? What factors affected the team spirit in your group? Would you do anything differently next time?

2   How well did your group use its time?

3   How well did you work together as a team? Did you make decisions collectively?

4   Did you allow one member to dominate the group, so preventing other members from contributing fully?

5   Were there any conflicts between group members? How well were they handled?

6   What can you do next time to improve the success of your group?

7   How would you rate the quality of the final presentation?

8   What can you avoid doing next time in order to improve the success of your group?

Go to the checklist on p.177. Look again at the tips relating to Unit 2 Parts A–C and tick (✓) those you have used in your studies. Read the tips relating to Unit 2 Part D.

Reporting in writing

By the end of Part E you will be able to:

- understand plagiarism
- paraphrase text
- summarize text
- use quotations.

1 Understanding plagiarism

1a Work in pairs. Discuss what you know about *plagiarism*. Then read the text and check your answers.

> *Plagiarism* means copying parts of the materials we refer to when writing an academic paper, without giving an acknowledgement. Plagiarism is often committed unintentionally by students who are not confident about expressing in their own words the information they read and hear. This is particularly true of students who are studying in a second or foreign language.
>
> Sections of text and ideas are considered to be private property in the same way that physical possessions are the property of the owner. One's academic ideas and text should not be used by another without acknowledging where they came from. Whether done intentionally or not, plagiarism is a very serious offence in the academic world and is considered a form of academic theft. At times, it is quite difficult to decide what *is* and what *is not* plagiarism.

1b Work in pairs. Discuss the writing approaches (1–13) listed in the table below. Decide whether each one is plagiarism (P), acceptable (A) or inappropriate (I). Note that 'inappropriate' means that although the approach is not 'academic theft', it is not good practice.

Approach	A/P/I
1 Copying a whole paragraph from another text without making changes or acknowledging the source	*P*
2 Finding a nice way of expressing an idea in another text and using it in your own writing	
3 Working with a friend who helps you with your assignment	
4 Reading an essay someone else has written and using some of their ideas without citing	
5 Finding an example of a good argument on a topic, and using the same argument but completely rewriting it in your own words	*A (if cited)*
6 Working with a partner from a different class and handing in similar essays	
7 Finding an essay on the Internet on the same topic and using some of it in your essay	
8 Including a fact that is generally well known without providing a reference	
9 Finding an interesting summary from another source and changing some of the words but without providing a citation in your essay	
10 Memorizing a passage from a text and writing it word for word in a timed exam	

11 Working on a project with a group, and handing in similar (but not identical) assignments	
12 Finding an essay on a similar topic in your own language, translating it and using it in your assignment	
13 Seeing a quotation in a text and using it in an assignment, citing the original writer but not the source	

When you write an academic paper, you need to use information from different sources to support your arguments and to give examples. However, you need to make sure that this type of information is acknowledged properly.

Sources of information are acknowledged in a piece of writing in two ways: *citations* and *references*.

1 **Citation**, i.e. a brief reference to sources of information within the main body of a text. The citation should appear at the point in the text where the information appears. Citations can be used with quotations, paraphrases and summaries.

   Examples
   Quotation with citation
   Saumell (2008, p.23) points out that 'few companies survive for longer than a century in their original form'.

   Paraphrase with citation
   Saumell (2008, p.23) points out that it is uncommon for a business to survive in its original form for longer than a hundred years.

   Summary with citation
   Saumell (2008) argues that change is common in long-lived businesses.

2 **Reference**, i.e. an entry in a list of all the sources of information referred to in your piece of work, provided at the very end of the piece of writing.

   Example
   Saumell, A. (2008). *Business: a guide*. Birmingham: Caulfield.

The References section gives full details of the sources of information used in your writing. The details included in this section vary according to the type of publication referred to (e.g. a book, an article, an internet site, etc.) but, where possible, usually include:

   - the name of the author
   - the date of publication
   - the exact title of the publication
   - who the publisher was
   - where it was published.

Learning how to acknowledge sources in your work is an important step towards making your writing more academically acceptable.

2 Paraphrasing text

2a Work in pairs. Discuss why it is important to avoid using phrases or passages from another author's words directly in your writing.

2b Discuss what you already know about paraphrasing. Then read the information below and check your answers.

> Paraphrasing is one approach writers can take to restate an idea from a phrase or passage in another author's work. The writer should provide a citation, and significantly change the language that the original author used.
>
> There is no fixed length for a paraphrase. It can be longer or shorter depending on the needs of your writing. But in all cases, you need to follow these steps to make an effective paraphrase.
>
>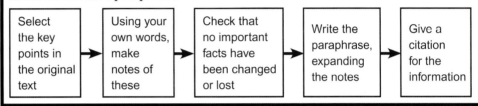
>
> | Select the key points in the original text | → | Using your own words, make notes of these | → | Check that no important facts have been changed or lost | → | Write the paraphrase, expanding the notes | → | Give a citation for the information |

2c Read this text on global warming. Below are four attempts to use the ideas in the text in academic work. Work in pairs. Decide which attempts are plagiarized and which are acceptable paraphrases. Make notes of the reasons for your decisions.

> The earth's climate is immensely complicated, far beyond our present understanding and the calculating powers of modern computers. Changes in phase from ice to water to vapour; cloud formation; convection; ocean currents; winds; changes in the sun; the complicated shapes of the land masses; the ability of the oceans to absorb carbon dioxide – all of these and a thousand other factors operating with small differences over vast masses and distances make it practically impossible for us to make predictions about long-term climate patterns, and perhaps make such predictions inherently impossible.
>
> ───────────
>
> Kenny, A. (2002, June) Preparing for The Big Chill, *The Spectator*, 289. Retrieved from http://www.spectator.co.uk/essays/10104/prepare-for-the-big-chill.thtml/

1 Kenny (2002) claims that the earth's climate is too complex and contains too many variables to allow reasonable predictions about future changes in the earth's climate to be made.

2 The earth's climate is extremely complicated, much beyond our current understanding and the powers of the latest computers. Variations in phase from ice to water to vapour; cloud formation; convection; sea currents; winds; changes in the sun; the complex shapes of the continents; the ability of the oceans to absorb CO_2 – all of these and many other factors operating with tiny differences over huge masses and distances make it almost impossible for us to make predictions about long-term weather patterns, and perhaps make these predictions inherently impossible (Kenny, 2002).

3 It has been argued that due to the extreme complexity of the world's climate we are unable to use computers to model its changes. There are so many possible factors such as currents in the ocean or changes in the sun that predicting future climate patterns is effectively impossible.

4   In attempting to predict future climatic trends there are many variables to consider, such as the take-up of carbon dioxide by the seas and the effects of ocean currents. Kenny (2002) argues that the complexity of these, combined with the limitations of computing power, means that useful predictions cannot be made.

	Plagiarized/Acceptable?	Why?
Text 1		
Text 2		
Text 3		
Text 4		

A paraphrase should:
• be in your own words
• support your ideas
• come from your notes of the original text
• keep the meaning of the original text the same, whilst using different language
• cite the original text
• show clearly where the paraphrase begins and ends.

2d Work in pairs. Discuss which of the paraphrases in 2c you think is best. Why?

2e Read this text and underline the key information.

Changing patterns of news consumption

According to a recent study by the Pew Research Centre (2009), in the last ten years the percentage of Americans getting news from a radio broadcast has fallen sharply. At the same time, there has been a 20% drop in the number of people reading a newspaper. In 2008, remarkably, more Americans got news from the Internet than from newspapers.

Another significant finding of the research is that many young people do not read any news at all. In addition, most people who read news on an internet site expect it to be available free. Traditionally, newspapers and television news programmes consisted of a package of news, comment, sport and entertainment. But today specialized websites that only provide a limited range of news, such as financial news or sports reports, are becoming popular.

Allison, R. (2009, February 17). Changing patterns of news consumption. Finance News Weekly, p.11.

2f Use the key information you underlined in 2e to paraphrase the text.

Paraphrase of 'Changing patterns of news consumption'
Modern media have changed the way people get the news. Allison (2009) provides evidence to show that ...

3   Summarizing text

Summarizing, in both writing and speech, is an important skill in any language. Summarizing is distinct from paraphrasing; paraphrasing involves restating an author's ideas, but not changing the original meaning. A paraphrase is usually the same length as the original text, either a sentence or paragraph. In contrast, when summarizing, a student focuses on an author's main idea, condensing key points from a longer text. A summary can be any length (but brief is preferable) and should not contain any of the student's own ideas. In academic work, summarizing is a key skill which is needed in many situations, e.g. giving a conclusion to a presentation, or stating writers' key ideas.

3a Work in pairs. Read the advice about writing a summary and decide whether the suggestions are correct (✓) or wrong (✗).

When writing a summary of a text, you should …

1 Read the text at least twice before writing the summary.

2 Make notes in your own words of main points from the original text.

3 Write the summary directly from the original text.

4 Include plenty of varied detail.

5 Include identified main points and any important supporting details.

6 Introduce new and interesting ideas, opinions and judgements of your own into the summary.

7 Retain the position and structure of each sentence but change some of the key words.

8 Change the order and structure of sentences if possible and, where possible, substitute new key words.

9 Revise the summary for incorrect inclusions, omissions, poor logical structure, language errors and missing references.

10 Check that the summary is about the same number of words as the original text, or a little longer if necessary.

3b Work in pairs. Read this text and the three summaries of the main idea that follow. Identify which summary follows the correct advice on p.79.

The postal service in Britain

Today communication by phone or email is so easy and convenient that we tend to forget the importance of letters in earlier periods, when travel was slower and they were the only means of sending news. The Post Office was originally set up to carry mail for members of the royal family only, but in 1635 the king, Charles I, permitted the general public to use the service. However, the early post was expensive, and the cost was based on the distance a letter had to travel. As a result, only the rich could afford to use the service, which was usually paid for by the recipient of a letter, not the sender. The idea of pre-payment was first used for letters inside London in 1680, when a penny was charged, and this pattern then spread to other cities.

However, the greatest change came about in 1840, when Rowland Hill introduced the penny post. His aim was to have a national postal system which was cheap enough for anyone to use. He realised that letters should just be charged by weight, rather than the distance they had to travel, so that the same price applied to all letters sent anywhere in the country. The other novel idea was the adhesive postage stamp, which Hill developed from ideas collected in a national competition. The world's first stamp, called the Penny Black, soon became famous. The final development in the system was the introduction of the letter box in 1852, which allowed people to post letters at any time, confident that they would be collected and delivered by the next day.

Levin, J. (2008). *The postal service in Britain*. London: Brunswick, p.4.

1 Nowadays it is so easy to phone that letters are not important. Emails are quicker and cheaper. The postal service was started for the king, but became more popular when Penny Black stamps were invented by Hill in 1840. Letter boxes were then used to collect the letters day and night (Levin, 2008, p.4).

2 In the seventeenth century the national mail service was expensive, and letters were paid for on delivery. The idea of pre-paid letters began in the large cities at the end of this century, but it was not until 1840 that a national service began, having a pre-payment system using penny stamps, with letter boxes following in 1852 (Levin, 2008, p.4).

3 In the past letters were priced according to distance, but a flat rate was first introduced in the nineteenth century. A letter could be sent to any address in the country for a penny. This was a much simpler system, and became very popular, especially when letter boxes were invented later (Levin, 2008, p.4).

3c Using the correct suggestions in 3a, summarize this text in about 50 words.

Early newspapers

Newspapers have been published in Britain for over 300 years, beginning at the start of the eighteenth century with the Norwich Post in 1701. A year later the first London paper appeared, and by 1709 nineteen papers were being published in London. Soon every town and city had at least one title. Many of these early newspapers only had a short life, and all had small circulations by modern standards: 2,000 copies might be sold weekly in a large city.

This was partly because of the limited size of most provincial towns, but mainly due to the high tax that the government put on newspapers: four pence per copy at the end of the century. This meant that the cheapest paper cost five pence, which was too expensive for ordinary people to afford. As a result, copies of a newspaper were often shared by up to twenty or more; they were read in coffee houses and pubs, and special clubs were set up for buying and reading them. As a result many more people had access to a daily or weekly newspaper than the circulation figures would indicate.

Evans, D.H. & Hewson, P. (2010). *No Line on the Horizon*. Dublin: Philanthropy Press, p.207.

Summary of 'Early newspapers'

3d Compare your summary with a partner.

4 Using quotations

In some situations, you may decide that instead of summarizing or paraphrasing the source text, it would be more effective to use the original writer's actual words. This is known as *quoting*.

Example
Original text (Frankland, 2009)
Communicating the importance of climate change to the public is a critical task.

Paraphrase of Frankland's work
According to Frankland (2009), it is vital to communicate to the public why climate change is so important. *

Quote of Frankland's work
According to Frankland, it is 'a critical task' (2009, p.137) to communicate to the public why climate change is so important.

Before you choose to use a quote, however, you should always ask yourself exactly why you are quoting rather than using a paraphrase.

* A citation must always include the name of the author and the year of publication. If the citation is used with a quotation or a specific piece of information that can be located within a text, a page number should also be added. If the citation refers to a more general idea or summary of a whole text, page numbers do not always appear.

4a Tick (✓) which of the following would be appropriate reasons for quoting an original text.

1 The language used in the original is correct: if you rewrote it in your own words, you might make it incorrect.

2 The original uses much more effective words than you could use.

3 The original version is a stronger or more important reference than a paraphrase or summary could be.

4 The original words express the information in such a concise way that it would be impossible to change them without making the reference much longer.

5 The exact meaning of the original is not clear, so it would be safer to quote the statement than risk misinterpreting it in a summary or paraphrase.

6 The original words express the information in such a precise way that if they were changed, the meaning of the statement would also change.

7 It's usually much easier to quote the actual words used as it isn't necessary to explain what they mean.

8 It's important to include as many quotations as possible to show the reader that you have referred to many different sources in your research and are not simply giving your own opinions.

9 It's important to increase the number of sources listed in your bibliography and including a lot of quotations is an easy way of doing this.

If, after very careful consideration, you decide to use a quotation instead of a summary or paraphrase, it is vital that you incorporate the quotation into your own writing.

You should not
✗ simply add the quotation to the end of a paragraph and let the reader work out why you have used it
✗ quote a long section of text without any of your own comment or analysis.

You should
✓ introduce the quotation and clearly indicate why you are using it
✓ clearly comment on the quotation and relate it to the point you are making
✓ give a source citation including name, year and page number.

A quotation needs to be introduced by a phrase which shows the source.

Example
Kenny argues that the global climate is too complex to make predictions because it is 'immensely complicated, far beyond our present understanding and the calculating powers of modern computers' (2002, p.97).

Note the normal pattern:

Name	Verb	Paraphrase	Quotation	Reference
Kenny	argues	that … predictions	'immensely … computers'	(2002, p.97)

Reporting verbs are often used to introduce quotations, e.g. *argue/claim*.

4b Can you think of any other reporting verbs?

Anything you write should be an original piece of work created almost entirely by you. It is acceptable to include short quotations from other authors' work, but these must always be accompanied by two things: clear quotation marks (" " or ' ') and a correct citation. Longer quotations do not use quotation marks, but should be indented, or printed in italics or smaller type.

Example
Kenny argues that the global climate is too complex to make predictions:

> *The earth's climate is immensely complicated, far beyond our present understanding and the calculating powers of modern computers. Changes in phase from ice to water to vapour; cloud formation; convection; ocean currents; winds; changes in the sun; the complicated shapes of the land masses; the ability of the oceans to absorb carbon dioxide – all of these and a thousand other factors operating with small differences over vast masses and distances make it practically impossible for us to make predictions about long-term climate patterns, and perhaps make such predictions inherently impossible. (Kenny, 2002, p.97)*

It is a fairly common mistake to include a long quotation from another author, but not to identify it by either of these methods. This may seem like a very small thing, but without the quotation marks your teacher may not consider it a quotation, and you may be accused of plagiarism.

4c Read this paragraph from the same text on global warming and answer these questions.

1 According to Kenny, how likely is another ice age?
2 How often do ice ages occur?
3 Is the recurrence of ice ages predictable?
4 How serious would another ice age be?

If the global warming scare has little foundation in fact, the ice age scare is only too solidly founded. For the last two million years, but not before, the Northern hemisphere has gone through a regular cycle of ice ages: 90,000 years with ice, 10,000 years without. The last ice age ended 10,000 years ago. Our time is up. The next ice age is due. What causes the ice ages? It is probably something to do with the shape and arrangement of northern land masses and the path of the Gulf Stream, but we do not know for sure. However, a new ice age, unlike global warming, would be a certain calamity.   (Kenny, 2002, p.97)

4d Following the pattern above, write your opinion on one of the following points and support it with a quote from Kenny:

1 The likelihood of another ice age

2 The frequency of ice ages

3 The predictability of ice ages

4 The impact of a new ice age on human life

Notes
Kenny states that 

> **UNIT TASK** **Modern media**

In this unit task, you will write an essay of 400–450 words with this title:

What are the most important sources of news for young people today?

a Write your essay plan below.

Plan for: What are the most important sources of news for young people today?

b Wherever possible, use paraphrasing, summarizing and quotations to support your arguments. You should refer to your sources (e.g. Newspaper Research Foundation, 2007) but you do not need to worry too much about the format of the bibliography at the end as you will do more work on this later.

 Go to the checklist on p.177. Look again at the tips relating to Unit 2 Parts A–D and tick (✓) those you have used in your studies. Read the tips relating to Unit 2 Part E.

Unit 3 Science and technology in society

Unit overview

Part	This part will help you to …	By improving your ability to …
A	**Follow lectures**	• understand signposting in lectures • identify restatement • predict content from language cues.
B	**Understand and use academic texts**	• reflect on challenges in academic reading • read for a purpose • read for detailed information • use sources to support your ideas.
C	**Find and evaluate sources of information**	• evaluate sources • evaluate a range of texts • use sources effectively • use headings and subheadings to locate information • use contents pages to locate information • use index pages to locate information.
D	**Deliver an academic presentation**	• understand what makes a good presentation • organize a presentation according to its purpose • use visual aids in a presentation • design appropriate visual aids.
E	**Create a piece of academic writing**	• create thesis statements • identify different essay structures • develop a topic sentence • develop ideas in writing.

Understanding spoken information

By the end of Part A you will be able to:

- understand signposting in lectures
- identify restatement
- predict content from language cues.

1 Understanding signposting in lectures

1a Match the pictures (1–5) with the ancient sites (a–e).

a Angkor Wat

What: Angkor was the world's largest pre-industrial city, covering an area of about 1,000 square kilometres. Larger than modern-day New York, ancient Angkor is thought to have had a population of 750,000.

Where: Angkor, Cambodia, South-East Asia

When: built by Khmer civilization between AD 802 and 1220

Why: built for King Suryavarman II, as his state temple and capital city

b Macchu Picchu

What: the 'lost city of the Incas' (about 34 square kilometres)

Where: on a mountain ridge, 2,400 metres above sea level, Peru, South America

When: around 1460

Why: built for the Inca rulers

c Midhowe Broch

What: a stone tower

Where: on the coast of Orkney, Scotland (there are 500 other Brochs around Scotland)

When: some time in the last centuries BC

Why: nobody is sure: just for show or as a defensive structure?

d The Terracotta Army

What: an army of statues made out of terracotta and buried underground: 7,000 infantry, 130 chariots with horses and 110 cavalry horses

Where: near Xi'an, Shaanxi province, China

When: built between 246 and 210 BC, over 2,200 years ago

Why: as an army to protect the First Qin Emperor in the afterlife

e Vinland

What: an ancient Viking settlement

Where: L'Anse aux Meadows, Northern Newfoundland, Canada

When: built in 11th century, around 400 years before Christopher Columbus 'discovered' America

Why: by accident: in one story, the Viking explorer Leif Ericson sailed off-course and landed in L'Anse aux Meadows, which he named Vinland due to the grapes that grew there

1b Work in pairs. Answer these questions.

1 Which site(s) was used by the rulers of civilizations?

2 Which site(s) is near the sea?

3 Which site(s) is built high above sea level?

4 Which site(s) was meant for a dead person?

5 Which site(s) do we know least about?

6 Which site(s) is the biggest?

7 Which site(s) suggests that 'accepted' history is wrong?

1c Work in pairs and compare sites 1–5. Answer these questions.

1 Which site do you find most interesting? Why?

2 Do you have anything similar in your country?

3 Have you ever visited one of the sites or somewhere similar?

1d Angkor Wat has been in ruins for several hundred years. Work in pairs. Discuss why you think the civilization which built it may have declined.

3.1

1e Listen to an extract from a lecture on the history of Angkor Wat. Answer these questions.

1 What two possible reasons for the decline of Angkor Wat are mentioned?

a _____

b _____

2 Why does the lecturer question reason a?

3 What problem did modern scientists face when researching reason b?

4 How did the scientists try to solve this problem?

5 Did their solution work?

> Speakers, including lecturers, have ways of helping the audience focus on the key points they are making.
>
> The speaker can use *signposting* language – particular words and expressions – to help listeners understand the structure and content of the talk more easily.

1f Before you listen to the next extract from the lecture, match the signposting phrases (1–7) in the table on p.88 with their purposes (a–g).

a define a term

b remind the audience of something previously said

c introduce a problem

d give a possible response

e suggest more evidence needs to be considered

f introduce an alternative response

g signal the conclusion

Signposting phrase	Purpose of phrase	Signposting phrase	Purpose of phrase
1 Well, to wind up …		5 Well, the obvious question is …	
2 I hope this case reinforces the point I made earlier …		6 Some people have suggested that …	
3 … which is …	a	7 So there's another possibility …	
4 But that can't be the whole answer.			

1g Check your answers with a partner.

3.2

1h You are going to listen to the next part of the lecture, which gives more detail about the reasons for the decline of Angkor Wat. Before you listen, read the transcript below and try to predict when the speaker will use the signposting phrases (1–7) from 1f. Listen to check your answers and complete a–g.

a_____ , what makes these droughts happen?

b_____ they are caused by El Niño, c_____
a fairly regular warming of the eastern Pacific Ocean. d_____,
because El Niño only lasts for a year or two, while the tree ring data shows that
the eighteenth-century drought lasted over 30 years. e_____
that the researchers have been looking at, which is the temperature of the
Indian Ocean, which can have an effect on the strength of the monsoons.

f_____, g_____, that it's very difficult to
pinpoint exact causes in a field as complex as climate change.

1i In this talk, the lecturer uses a problem–solution structure like the one you studied in Unit 2 Part B, section 4e. Look at the transcript for the first part of the lecture about south-east Asia (**Appendix 5**).

1 Identify the four different parts of the problem–solution structure.

2 Underline the words and phrases which are used to introduce the different parts of the structure.

2 Identifying restatement

2a Look at the phrases in italics below. What is the speaker doing in each case?

• … a long drought, *when monsoon rainfall was well below normal.*

• … suffered from dyspraxia, *a medical condition which affects people's ability to perform physical actions.*

• … it's an evergreen, *a kind of tree which has leaves all year round.*

Speakers often give definitions or explanations of new words or phrases immediately after saying them. This technique is known as *restatement*, and can be very useful to identify as it gives the listener a second chance to check their understanding of a concept.

2b You are going to listen to a short talk which gives information about the weather phenomenon El Niño. Work in pairs and use the words and map below to discuss where El Niño occurs and what weather is connected with it.

drought   flooding   heavy rain   Pacific Ocean   rising air pressure

sea   temperature   tropical storms   winds

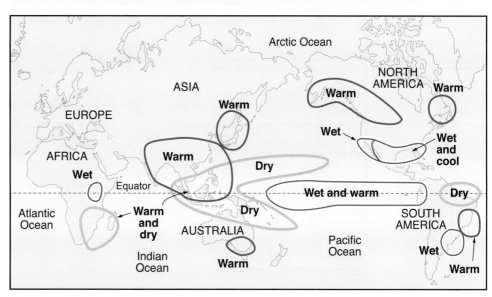

Figure 1: Weather conditions during an El Niño year

3.3

2c Listen to the talk and check your ideas about El Niño.

2d Listen again. This time, write notes to help you define the expressions below.

	Expression	Notes
1	ENSO	
2	oscillation	
3	trade winds	
4	lag behind	
5	La Niña	

2e Check your answers with a partner.

3 Predicting content from language cues

A listener can often predict the general content or purpose of what the speaker will say next from the use of certain language cues. For example, if the lecturer says, *It is often claimed that television was invented in Britain. However,* ... we can predict that the next sentence will give an opposing viewpoint.

These are some of the most common language cues and their functions.

Language cue	Function	
secondly, next, then, finally	1	To order ideas
on the other hand, but, despite that, yet	2	To show opposition
in other words, that is to say, I'll put that another way	3	To show restatement
crucially, significantly, above all, critically	4	To give emphasis
although, nevertheless, whereas, while, however	5	To show an alternative viewpoint
as a result, consequently, that's why	6	To show cause and effect
a case in point, specifically, namely	7	To introduce an example
by the way, incidentally	8	To mark an anecdote or side issue
in a few words, to sum up, in conclusion	9	To summarize or conclude

3.4

3a Listen to six statements (a–f) and write which of the categories (1–9) from the table above each statement belongs to.

Statement	Category
a	*6*
b	
c	
d	
e	
f	

3b What do you know about electric cars? Work in pairs. Complete the table below and discuss the advantages and disadvantages of electric cars versus petrol-powered cars.

	Electric cars	Petrol-powered cars
Cost		
Performance		
Noise		
Effect on environment		

3.5

3c Listen to a lecture called *Socializing the electric car*. The first time you listen, you will not hear the complete lecture as some sections have been deleted. Take notes on what you hear.

Socializing the electric car

3d The deleted sections of the lecture are introduced by the phrases in the table below. How much of the deleted content can you predict from these prompts? Complete the phrases with a logical conclusion in the second column of the table.

Previous phrase	Prediction
1 Firstly, they are cheaper to run. Secondly, …	
2 There is clearly a demand for …	
3 However, there is a …, which is the danger to pedestrians and cyclists	
4 … when the cars are travelling at slow speeds; in other words …	
5 … being studied in various countries, for example …	
6 a number of benefits, but also …	

3.6

3e Listen to the complete lecture and check your predictions from 3d.

3f Focus on the structure of the lecture as a whole. Listen again and answer these questions.

1 Can you identify a problem–solution pattern?

2 According to the lecturer, is the proposed solution likely to be successful?

3 How far do you agree with the points made in the lecture?

3g You are going to discuss this topic:

Electric cars are too expensive and will never be economically viable as a substitute for petrol-powered cars.

Work in two groups. Group A – discuss only arguments which support this claim. Group B – discuss only arguments which contradict this claim.

3h Change groups so you are working with somebody who discussed the other side of the argument. Introduce all your points, and then discuss which argument is the strongest.

> **UNIT TASK** **Packaging and waste**

The Unit 3 task is about packaging and waste. At the end of each part, you will be asked to complete a stage of the task as follows:

Part A: Listen to an introduction on the topic.

Part B: Read a text about it.

Part C: Do some further research for relevant material.

Part D: Give a short presentation on the topic.

Part E: Write an essay with this title:

'In 2008, an estimated 10.7 million tonnes of packaging waste was disposed of in the UK (Department of Environment, Food and Rural Affairs, 2008). If this continues, the environmental impact could be catastrophic.'

Discuss the problems associated with disposing of large amounts of waste, then identify different ways of reducing the amount of waste people produce. In your essay, you should refer to a number of sources and can include your own ideas on this topic. Try to provide a list of references at the end. The essay should be approximately 750 words.

To start your research you will look at how modern methods of packaging reduce the amount of waste that society produces, looking at the advantages and disadvantages of different types of packaging material.

a　You are going to listen to a short talk comparing the environmental impacts of paper and plastic shopping bags. Work in pairs. Discuss some of the things you think might be mentioned. Write some notes which you think will help you listen to the talk.

The environmental impact of paper and plastic shopping bags

b　Listen to the talk and complete your notes.

3.7

c　Were your pre-listening notes helpful? Think about how they might be made more helpful.

Go to the checklist on p.178 and read the tips relating to Unit 3 Part A.

Unit 3
Part B — Understanding written information

By the end of Part B you will be able to:
- reflect on challenges in academic reading
- read for a purpose
- read for detailed information
- use sources to support your ideas.

1 Challenges in academic reading

1a One of the biggest problems students have at college or university is the sheer amount and complexity of reading they need to do. Read what four students have to say about their reading and underline the problems.

When I first started university, I was overwhelmed by the amount that I had to read. I just couldn't keep up. It was really difficult to read so much and I couldn't follow lectures or tutorials. After a while, I spoke to some friends about my problems and they told me to make a timetable of reading. Now I am much better organized. I still find that there is a lot of reading but now I can understand my studies a lot more.

Shayan, 25, Iran

I had a real problem with understanding what I needed to read. I had to understand every single word or I would get really anxious about missing something important. Because I was trying hard to understand everything, I ended up understanding nothing. I couldn't sleep because it made me so worried. My friend and I took extra reading classes and we were taught how to skim and scan and select what was important to read. I think that this is an important skill: being able to decide what not to concentrate on. Sometimes there is just too much to read so you have to be selective. I am a lot more relaxed about reading now and a lot more confident too. Now, I don't get panic attacks if I don't read everything.

Fei Fei, 24, China

When I first started studying at university, I used to accept that what I was reading was the truth. It was a big shock to me when my teacher said that I have to think more about my reading. I thought that if I just said what other people wrote then I would be fine. But I wasn't getting good marks. I spoke to my tutor and she told me to think critically about what I read and to question things, like what is the author's position or what information did the writer leave out? When I started thinking about this it helped me understand my subject more and my marks started improving.

Olivia, 21, Nigeria

I found lots of things difficult when I first started university. I feel that I can speak well and I can listen but reading, for me, was one of the toughest things I had to do. I just couldn't take anything in. I could read for ages but if someone asked me about it I could not have told them. It was really frustrating doing all this reading and not taking any of it in. I spoke to my student advisor and they suggested that I have a clear purpose before I read. For example, I ask myself a question and then read an article to find out the answer. I didn't always find an answer but I found that I became more focused on my reading and I was able to understand and talk about what I had read. I would recommend to anyone wanting to study at university to have a clear idea of what kind of information you are looking for before you read something.

Omar, 23, Saudi Arabia

1b Work in pairs. Read the texts in 1a again and find solutions to each student's problem.

1c Work in pairs. Discuss these questions.

1   Are any of the students' experiences similar to yours?

2   Have you tried any of the suggested solutions? If so, did you find them useful?

3   Would you suggest any other solutions?

2   Reading for a purpose

2a Why is it important to do so much reading in higher education? Put these reasons in order of importance for you. Can you add any reasons of your own?

To find information for your studies ☐

For pleasure ☐

To learn new things ☐

To prepare for assessments and exams ☐

2b Compare your answers with a partner. How similar are your lists?

> The first step in becoming an efficient reader is to be clear about why you are reading something. If you don't know why you are reading something, then it is difficult to focus on the task and you may be wasting your time. Be clear about what you are looking for.

2c Look at this list of text types and decide why you might want to read each one. Write notes in the table.

| advertisement | essay | journal article | logbook | magazine article |
| newspaper | poster | report | textbook | website |

Reason for reading	Text type
to obtain facts	
to read a balanced argument	
to prepare for an exam or assignment	
to find a solution to a problem	
to find important information	
to compare different items or ideas	
to read about the effects of something	
to obtain non-specialist information	

2d Your tutor has given you this discussion task:

Identify and explain some methods of reducing the effects of global warming.

Work in pairs. Discuss what issues connected with global warming you are aware of. Write notes below.

Issues connected with global warming

2e You are going to read three texts which focus on specific issues connected with global warming. Skim the texts on pp.96–98. Which text discusses

1 methods for reducing carbon dioxide emissions?

2 alternative types of domestic lighting?

3 ways of reducing climate change?

2f Work in small groups. Each group should select one of the three texts. Before reading the text again, discuss and note your own ideas for resolving your chosen issue.

Issues connected with global warming	Ways of resolving the issue
Rising temperatures	
High levels of carbon dioxide	
Use of electric light bulbs	

2g Read your chosen text again and compare it with your own solutions.

3　Reading for detailed information

3a　Skim read your chosen text again and tick (✓) which of these ideas you find.

1　The cost of different solutions

2　Approaches in different countries

3　Solutions using existing technology

4　Responses that are unlikely to work

5　Methods to reduce CO_2

6　Problems with the technology

Space umbrellas and artificial clouds

Geo-engineering is a new branch of science, concerned with reducing the effects of global warming. It is based on the theory that cutting the emissions of carbon dioxide into the atmosphere will not happen fast enough to delay the harmful consequences of rising temperatures. Therefore mankind should experiment with large-scale engineering projects which would help to cool the planet. One proposal, for instance, is a giant floating parasol, which would act like a blanket of cloud to shade parts of the earth from the sun.

Various similar suggestions have been studied in a recent paper published in *Atmospheric Chemistry and Physics Discussions* (Lenton and Vaughan, 2009). The aim of this study was to evaluate the likely effectiveness of the projects, without regard to their cost. They found that the solar umbrella, even if ways could be found to keep it positioned high above the earth, would have to be half the size of Brazil (four million square kilometres) merely in order to counterbalance half the expected warming over the next century. Clearly, building and maintaining such a structure would be an immensely challenging task.

Another idea is to inject sulphate particles into the stratosphere, since they would reflect some of the sun's rays back into space, in the same way that a major volcanic eruption can cause a temporary cooling in the earth's climate. But even this, they calculate, would not compensate for more than half of the expected warming. Moreover, the sulphate particles would not last for more than a few years so would need replacing regularly.

Creating clouds artificially by spraying seawater into the atmosphere is a third possibility, and the scientists believe it would have a similar effect to using particles, but might be more difficult technically.

The paper also discusses the likely side-effects of these schemes, which might have severe and unpredictable environmental consequences. Another plan, for example, aimed to pour iron into the sea in order to encourage the growth of carbon-eating phytoplankton, a tiny sea creature. However, there are fears that, if successful, this might consume all the oxygen in those parts of the ocean and thereby kill all other sea creatures. An experiment to test this theory was recently stopped by the German government, who feared it might be illegal under international law. It seems that there are no easy answers in this area.

Markovic, T. (2009). Space Umbrellas and Artificial Clouds, *Geo-engineering Today*, *3* (2), 33–39.

Sky cleaning?

There is now general agreement that levels of carbon dioxide (CO_2) in the atmosphere have risen significantly in the last hundred years and are a major factor in the increase in average temperatures. Consequently, many countries have encouraged the adoption of low-carbon technologies such as wind or solar power, with the aim of lowering their production of so-called 'greenhouse gases'. But some scientists are now claiming that a more direct way to reduce CO_2 levels is to set up plants which collect the gas from the air.

Small-scale versions of these machines already operate on board submarines, where they prevent CO_2 concentrations from reaching dangerous levels. Much larger models would collect the gas from the atmosphere and then sell it for industrial use, for example in food processing. These gas collecting machines could be sited anywhere in the world, so they could be near a source of cheap energy, such as a hydro-electric power station, or where carbon dioxide was needed.

Although the actual design of machines large enough to have an impact on CO_2 levels is still uncertain, supporters of this proposal have to answer three main objections. The first is technical: if the power needed to run these machines produces more emissions than is gained from the collection, then the project is pointless. The second consideration is financial: are there cheaper ways of reducing carbon dioxide levels, such as building wind farms? Finally, the political aspect needs considering, since building these plants might give other countries an excuse to increase their production of greenhouse gases.

Taking the technical issue first, the prototype plant appears to create emissions of under five per cent of the CO_2 collected, making it reasonably viable. But the financial aspect is more uncertain; unless the cost of building and running these machines could be hugely reduced, alternative methods of lowering carbon dioxide levels are much more economical. Similarly, the politics of carbon capture are unclear, so that unless there is a technical breakthrough in the process, it seems unlikely that large-scale machines will be worth building.

Dorman, C. (2010, July 25). Sky Cleaning?, *New Technologist*, 57–61.

The light of the world

The first light bulb, demonstrated by Thomas Edison in 1879, offered a huge improvement on gas lights, which were dirty and gave an inferior light. His incandescent bulb worked by heating a filament of wire in a vacuum inside a glass container, but this design had two drawbacks. Firstly it was inefficient, since only five per cent of the energy was turned into light, the rest being lost as heat, and additionally it only had a life of about 1,000 hours.

As a result, many countries are now replacing these with more energy-efficient compact fluorescent lights (CFL). These contain mercury vapour which is energized by the electric current, and use only 25% of the power of traditional bulbs, while lasting ten times longer. However, critics of these bulbs claim that the light quality is inferior, that they are slow to light up, and that there may be health risks. Additionally, CFL bulbs are more difficult to manufacture than the older ones, which makes them five or six times more expensive.

However, a more recent lighting technology, light-emitting diodes (LEDs), offer a significant improvement. They were first used as red indicator lights on electronic equipment, and then for car headlights and streetlights. Although very complex to produce, they are now being developed for domestic and commercial lighting. Their advantages are significant energy savings of over 75% and a much longer life, up to 45,000 hours. This is particularly beneficial for large organizations where the cost of paying for bulb replacement is significant.

However, LEDs still cost far more than alternative bulbs and most householders are unlikely to use them until the cost is substantially reduced. Work at Cambridge University is currently developing ways of cutting costs by using silicon rather than sapphire in the process. It has been estimated that if LEDs were cheap enough to be widely used it would cut demand for electricity by around ten per cent. In a country the size of the USA, for instance, this would mean needing a hundred less power stations. In addition, solar-powered LEDs could be used in areas without mains electricity, such as large parts of Africa, where oil lamps and candles are still the norm.

Hang, A. (2008). The light of the world, *Development Issues Quarterly*, 3 (12), 81–103.

3b Read your chosen text a third time and answer these questions.

1 What is the aim of the text?

2 How would you describe the writer's tone, e.g. positive/negative/balanced/ biased/cautious/arrogant/respectful/dismissive? Give examples.

3 How does the writer's tone affect the way you respond to the texts?

4 Is the writer simply stating facts, or do they give opinions or interpretations of the facts?

5 If opinions and interpretations are given, do you agree with them?

3c Check your answers in small groups.

3d Consider the structure of your text in more detail and answer these questions.

    1 **Situation** Where in the text is the situation stated?

    2 **Problem** Where is the problem stated?

    3 **Response** Where are responses proposed?

    4 **Evaluation** Where are these responses evaluated? Are they evaluated positively or negatively?

3e Complete the table below for your text, showing how the contents of each paragraph reflect the SPRE structure. How successfully do you think your text is organized?

	Function		
Paragraph	**Text A**	**Text B**	**Text C**
1			*Situation; Problem: incandescent bulbs are inefficient with a short life expectancy*
2	*Response: solar umbrella; Problem (negative evaluation)*		
3		*Problems x 3 – technical, financial, political*	
4			
5			

> This kind of analysis can be extended to all types of texts in your subject (although not all texts have SPRE structure). For example, if you are a science student and read a lot of reports, then you can work out quite easily how they are structured.

3f Work in groups of three with students who read different texts. Answer these questions.

    1 What ideas did the different texts put forward?

    2 What other information can you now add to this table?

    3 How similar is the paragraph structure of the three texts?

    4 Which text seems the most logically organized to you?

4 Using sources to support your ideas

4a In order to develop your ideas fully, it's a good idea to read and use a number of sources. Look at this paragraph from a student's essay. Which issue connected with global warming is the focus?

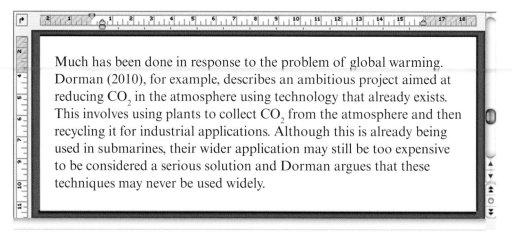

Much has been done in response to the problem of global warming. Dorman (2010), for example, describes an ambitious project aimed at reducing CO_2 in the atmosphere using technology that already exists. This involves using plants to collect CO_2 from the atmosphere and then recycling it for industrial applications. Although this is already being used in submarines, their wider application may still be too expensive to be considered a serious solution and Dorman argues that these techniques may never be used widely.

4b The student's paragraph can be divided into three parts:

    a The student's idea

    b Support from an expert source

    c Evaluation of idea (positive or negative).

Insert slashes (/) into the student's paragraph to show these three parts.

4c Check your answers with a partner.

4d Use the structure in 4a and information from texts A–C on pp.96–98 to develop three paragraphs to support the statements below in your own words. How can you introduce others' ideas into your argument?

    1 Another idea is to develop much larger-scale solutions.

    2 However, not all of these big ideas are practical.

    3 The best answers may be the simplest.

> **UNIT TASK** · **Packaging and waste**

In this unit task, you will research information on this title:

'In 2008, an estimated 10.7 million tonnes of packaging waste was disposed of in the UK (Department of Environment, Food and Rural Affairs, 2008). If this continues, the environmental impact could be catastrophic.'

Discuss the problems associated with disposing of large amounts of waste, then identify different ways of reducing the amount of waste people produce. In your essay, you should refer to a number of sources and can include your own ideas on this topic. Try to provide a list of references at the end. The essay should be approximately 750 words.

a   As part of your research into some of the issues you may want to include, read the article below and take notes about the dangers of the overuse of plastic bags.

b   Read the article again and answer these questions.

1   What is the main purpose of the text? Who is the text aimed at?

2   What information does the text present (advantages only, disadvantages only, both)?

3   How balanced is the text? Does it present a range of views, or one side only?

4   What is the structure of the article?

5   Where would you expect to find this article?

Environmental dangers of plastic bags
Sara Wittenberg. June 6th 2009

Plastics are not cheap and are environmentally costly and destructive
Plastic bags are used in vast numbers all over the world; they are extremely cheap, lightweight yet durable, and easily accessible. They became commonplace in the early 1980s, and today between 500 billion to one trillion are used annually. It is estimated that over one billion plastic bags are distributed free to consumers each day, and that in the United States alone over 100 billion are used every year. However, because of this extensive use, plastic bags are becoming an ever-increasing problem. Plastic bags, plastic bottles, and other synthetic materials have contributed to the world's biggest garbage dump, the Great Pacific Garbage Patch, in the Pacific Ocean.

The high cost of plastic bags
It is becoming increasingly obvious that plastic bags are an eyesore; China's streets are white with them, and they've earned the title 'white pollution'. South Africa bitterly dubs them the national flower due to their prevalence. Aesthetic reasons alone offer an incentive to clean up plastic bags. In the United States, an estimated eight billion pounds of plastic sacks are found in the annual waste. In 2002 in Australia, the countryside was littered with 50–80 million plastic bags. And contrary to popular belief, they are not free. The estimated annual cost to retailers in the USA is $4 billion, which the consumer ultimately pays for through higher product prices. They are made with petroleum, a non-renewable natural resource that is becoming increasingly in short supply and is often obtained from foreign countries, strengthening our dependence on these nations. They may be convenient, but they are neither cheap nor a good investment economically or ecologically.

Why plastic bags are a danger

Convenience for consumers translates into ecological hell for many of Earth's inhabitants. Plastic bags create massive amounts of pollution and they kill wildlife. Every year over one million marine mammals, reptiles, and birds succumb to death by plastic bags. Animals can become entangled in them, which may result in loss of limb or death, and they routinely ingest them. Many sea turtles (which are listed as threatened or endangered, depending on the species) eat a diet rich in jellyfish. Plastic bags look amazingly similar to jellyfish when floating in ocean currents, enticing animals to eat them, where they become lodged in their digestive tract, often leading to a slow and painful death. A study found that plastic bags were the number one material found in the digestive tracts of 400 dead leatherback turtles, appearing in over one-third of the animals.

Although plastic bags take up to one thousand years to decompose, through time they slowly disintegrate, soaking up toxic chemicals such as PCBs and DDE like sponges from the surrounding ocean water. As these plastics are ingested, the animals are not only eating gut-blockers but are also getting high doses of deadly synthetic compounds.

Solving the plastic bag problem

Ireland has instituted a 'PlasTax', adding a cost of twenty cents per bag; since March of 2002, the use of plastic bags has dropped by over ninety per cent. The Australian government instituted a voluntary programme for retailers to reduce the use of plastic bags, and over ninety per cent of retailers have signed up. Taiwanese law requires businesses to charge customers for plastic bags and utensils; as such, plastic product use has dropped by 69%. Many other countries and cities are being proactive in solving this overwhelming problem. Every time a plastic bag is avoided, the problem is improved. Reusable shopping bags are a viable solution to this serious problem. If everyone does their part, plastics in the environment could be decreased over time.

Go to the checklist on p.178. Look again at the tips relating to Unit 3 Part A and tick (✓) those you have used in your studies. Read the tips relating to Unit 3 Part B.

Part C Investigating

By the end of Part C you will be able to:

- evaluate sources
- evaluate a range of texts
- use sources effectively
- use headings and subheadings to locate information
- use contents pages and indexes to locate information.

1 Evaluating sources

In Unit 1, you learned how to locate source texts in your college or university library or online to help you complete assignments. You will often find many more sources than you actually need, and only parts of them may be suitable for your task.

The type of information you search for often depends on your purpose. Generally speaking, you choose information because it can help to develop your understanding or support your ideas and claims, but the standard of the evidence you choose depends on what you are using it for.

1a Match the situations (1–3) with appropriate sources of information in the box. More than one answer is possible for each situation.

1 You are having a discussion with a friend about safety in your city.

2 You are writing a research paper at university about crime levels.

3 You and some friends are planning a vacation in a foreign country and want to know if it's safe.

- 'common knowledge' – things you knew or believed already
- popular blog about the subject
- free encyclopedia such as Wikipedia
- government publication
- newspaper article
- academic journal
- popular magazine article
- primary research
- textbook
- TV documentary
- TV news broadcast
- specialist website

1b Work in pairs. Discuss how you might decide whether one source of information might be considered more suitable than another. Write your ideas below.

How to judge whether a text is suitable

Look at the date of publication – how old is the text? Is it still likely to be relevant?

3.8

1c Listen to this study skills teacher talking about evaluating sources. Add any new information to your notes.

1d You have been asked to write an essay with this title:

Outline the state of global exploration for oil at the beginning of the 21st century and relate this to likely future levels of production.

Having read and made notes on the sources from the reading list your tutor gave you, you have decided to do some further research. You entered the term 'oil exploration' in the library catalogue search engine and found these seven results. Use your notes in 1b to help you decide which sources are likely to be the most suitable.

	Title	Year
1	*Hydrocarbon exploration and production* / Frank Jahn, Mark Cook and Mark Graham	2nd ed. 2008
2	*China and the global energy crisis: development and prospects for China's oil and natural gas* / Tatsu Kambara, Christopher Howe	2007
3	*Deepwater petroleum exploration & production: a nontechnical guide* [electronic resource] / William L. Leffler, Richard Pattarozzi, Gordon Sterling	2003
4	*Soft computing and intelligent data analysis in oil exploration* [electronic resource] / edited by M. Nikravesh, F. Aminzadeh, L.A. Zadeh	2003
5	*Operational aspects of oil and gas well testing* [electronic resource] / Stuart McAleese	2000
6	*Oil and gas exploration in Derbyshire* [unpublished MEng dissertation] / Jenny Cook	1982
7	*Geophysical exploration: an outline of the principal methods used in the search for minerals, oil, gas and water supplies* / F.W. Dunning	1970

1e After searching in the library, you try looking online to find other sources. Work in pairs. Discuss which of the following you would choose to help you and why.

1 The home page of a major petroleum-producing company's website. The title of the page is 'Our business'. It was last updated six months ago.

2 An online magazine for the oil industry called 'Global Petroleum.com'.

3 A five-minute news broadcast from the BBC about oil production in Nigeria. It was posted online in 2000.

4 The Wikipedia page for 'Energy'. It was last updated two weeks ago.

5 A website about the global oil industry from an environmental organization called 'Go Solar Now.org'. It is updated daily.

6 An article called 'New Frontiers of Oil Exploration'. It is on a website hosted by a university, and was created in 2004.

7 A blog called 'Black Gold: discussions about our energy needs'.

8 The page for 'How Oil Drilling Works' on HowStuffWorks.com, a website started by a university professor in 1998 and now owned by Discovery Communications (owners of the Discovery Channel).

1f Before your next lesson, find at least two more websites you would recommend for this title.

2 Evaluating a range of texts

> Before reading to get information for an assignment, it can help if you ask yourself such questions as:
>
> - What do I already know about the subject? What points would I like to include in my assignment?
> - What is my opinion about the subject? (if applicable)
> - What information will I need to support these points / my opinion?
> - Am I only looking for information that supports these points, or other (perhaps opposing) ideas as well?
> - What is the scope of the information that I need? (e.g. is it about a single country or the world in general?)

2a You have been told to write an essay with this title:

Outline the social advantages and disadvantages of modern communication technology.

Work in pairs. Use the questions above to help you decide what information you might be looking for.

2b You have found three texts which you think might be relevant. However, a closer reading shows that none is suitable. Work in three groups. Members of each group should read one of the texts and decide why you wouldn't use this text. Write your reasons in the table below.

Text	Reasons
A	
B	
C	

A

Source: Book: *100 years of technological development* (2004). Chapter 4: The 1920s

One of the most striking aspects of the post-war period was the disappearance of servants from many middle-class homes. Maids and cooks became scarce, and when they were still found they could expect higher wages. It has been argued (Hare, 2001) that this trend was caused by the spread of household electrical equipment, such as the vacuum cleaner and the cooker. Certainly this was the period when many urban areas were connected to mains electricity, making possible the use of these labour-saving devices. However, the opposite view is presented by Gilbert and Leaviss (1998), who claim that the development of such machines was encouraged by the lack of servants, rather than the other way round. It seems that many women who had found independence in factory work during the First World War were reluctant to return to the bondage of domestic work afterwards, and this stimulated the production of the irons, toasters and fridges which were soon to become common.

B

Source: Website: The mobile plague (no author name). Accessed 23/05/11.

Few parts of the world are now free from mobile phones, from a dusty village in the Upper Nile valley to the passenger cabin of a jumbo jet high above the Pacific Ocean. It seems that everybody has at least one, and it's estimated that there are over six billion in use today. Since the first phones were produced in the early 1980s, they have become an essential item for business and pleasure, but at the same time they have made life noisier and less private. Railway carriages and restaurants are full of people having loud conversations about personal matters, to which other passengers and diners are forced to listen. Clearly, many people feel more secure carrying a mobile, knowing they can phone for help whenever they need to, but unfortunately many people also forget to turn them off in lectures, theatres and cinemas, so that the performances are often spoiled by noisy ringtones.

C

Source: Newspaper: July 15 2011 Story: Judge slams 'disgraceful' video game

After finding both defendants guilty, Lord Justice Booth criticized the video game 'Massive Kill' which he said had contributed to their dreadful crime. 'By encouraging young people to indulge in such horrible fantasies', he said, 'the makers are creating an irresponsible culture in which the impressionable young lose all touch with reality. After playing this lethal game for hours and hours these two went out deliberately looking for some innocent victim to attack.' The judge went on to say that the majority of players of video games were able to distinguish fact from fiction, but that for a small minority there was a real risk of being influenced to commit crimes, and that therefore this particular game should be banned. The makers of 'Massive Kill', The Massive Games Corporation, said in a press statement that there was no proven link between their products and any criminal activity, and that the vast majority of players were well-balanced and sociable young people.

2c Work with students from the other groups. Compare what you read and discuss the problems with the texts. Which of the texts seems the most/least useful overall? Why?

3 Using sources effectively

3a Look at these statements. Decide whether they are true (T) or false (F) about your approach to using sources.

1 When I have found a text which is connected to the subject, I just start reading and taking notes.

2 I identify parts of a text which are relevant and only read those parts.

3 I can only say I have 'used' a source if I have read it completely.

4 If I am using a book, I use the contents page to help me find the relevant sections, and only read those.

5 If I am using a book, I always use the index to locate useful information.

6 A 30-page source with only one page directly relevant to my topic is not useful.

7 I skim through a possible text first, and look at section headings, subheadings and any pictures or graphs to get an idea of which parts are relevant to me.

3b Check your answers with a partner and discuss any differences.

3c You are going to listen to a lecturer explaining how to read sources most effectively. Say which of the statements in 3a the lecturer might mention as being good techniques when finding information in a source.

3.9

3d Listen and take notes about the lecturer's advice.

Using source texts effectively

3e How do the answers you gave in 3a compare with the lecturer's advice?

4   Using headings and subheadings to locate information

> A key skill for using sources effectively is learning to use section headings, contents pages, and indexes within a text. This can save you a great deal of time and help you locate useful information.

4a You are writing a report on climate change. You want to find the following information.

1   Causes and effects of climate change

2   Possible ways to solve the problems that climate change causes

Turn to **Appendix 6**. Look at the headings and subheadings of the article on climate change. Which sections of the article are likely to contain the information that you need? Read only the sections that you think are useful and take notes.

Causes and effects	Possible solutions

4b Compare your notes with a partner.

5 Using contents pages

5a You find two more sources for your climate change report which might be relevant. Look at the contents page of each source below and answer these questions.

1 a Which source(s) will help you find information about global climate change?

   b What is the most relevant section of the source?

2 Which section of each source will help you learn about the causes and effects of climate change?

3 Which section deals with rising sea levels?

4 You want to include a section in your essay about possible solutions for climate change. Which sections of the two sources can help you get information for this?

A

Table of contents

1 Preface	1
2 Worldwide greenhouse gas emissions	4
3 Mitigation in the medium term (until 2025)	9
4 Mitigation in the long term (after 2025)	18
5 Policies and measures to mitigate climate change	20
6 Sustainable development and climate change mitigation	23
7 Gaps in knowledge	25

If you are unsure of the term *mitigation*, refer to **Appendix 6** on pp.190–191.

B

Energy, population, and climate change

a Acknowledgements	1
b Introduction: Population and climate change in the UK	4
c Scope of the problem	
• Energy consumption, changing demographics and climate change	6
d Potential climate change impacts on the UK population	
• Rising temperatures, changes in weather, rising sea levels, human health	10
e Details	
• Changes in land use, urbanization and household demographics	13
• Impacts of climate change on populations in coastal areas	15
• The relationship between climate change and population size	19
• The relationship between climate change and energy use	23
f Population and climate change by region	
• Europe, the Americas, Asia, Australasia, Africa, the Pacific	28
g Conclusion	57
h Endnotes	59

6 Using index pages to locate information

Before using an index page to search for a particular item, it can be useful to brainstorm associated words and ideas and check the index for these as well. Below, a student has used a mind map to brainstorm ideas related to the term *Independent learning*. Note how the brainstorm includes:

• synonyms for key terms, e.g. *studying, learning*

• related ideas, e.g. *using a library, time management*.

6a Can you add any more ideas to the mind map?

6b Work in pairs. Use a mind map to brainstorm these ideas.

1 Writing an essay/report

2 Doing research

6c Look at the index pages from a study skills book on pp.110–111 and answer these questions.

1 Which pages would you look at for advice on independent learning?

2 Which pages give advice about preparing for exams?

3 Where can you find information about using a computer?

4 Which pages will help you with writing an essay?

5 Where should you look if you are worried about exams?

Index

In this unit task, you will continue to research information for this title:

'In 2008, an estimated 10.7 million tonnes of packaging waste was disposed of in the UK (Department of Environment, Food and Rural Affairs, 2008). If this continues, the environmental impact could be catastrophic.'

Discuss the problems associated with disposing of large amounts of waste, then identify different ways of reducing the amount of waste people produce. In your essay, you should refer to a number of sources and can include your own ideas on this topic. Try to provide a list of references at the end. The essay should be approximately 750 words.

a Search for some more sources that you can use for your essay about packaging and waste. Find two other sources in the library or on the Internet.

b Bring extracts of your sources to share with other students. Explain why you feel each one is suitable for use in your essay.

Source 1	Source 2

Go to the checklist on p.178. Look again at the tips relating to Unit 3 Parts A–B and tick (✓) those you have used in your studies. Read the tips relating to Unit 3 Part C.

Reporting in speech

By the end of Part D you will be able to:

- understand what makes a good presentation
- organize a presentation according to its purpose
- use visual aids in a presentation
- design appropriate visual aids.

1 Understanding what makes a good presentation

1a Work in pairs. Read these statements and discuss whether you agree or disagree with each one.

1 If you have time to do so, it is better to write out the whole of your presentation so you can read it to the audience.

2 You should try to leave time for a question-and-answer session.

3 If you know about the subject you are presenting, there is no need to do any research.

4 If you have planned all the areas of your presentation, there is no need to rehearse it.

5 Giving a group presentation is easier than giving one on your own.

6 The best way of organizing a presentation is first to tell your audience what you are going to say, then to say it, and finally to summarize for your audience what you have just said.

7 You should let people ask you questions during the presentation if they wish to do so.

8 It is a good idea to sit down while you are giving your presentation.

9 If you have been given a time limit for your talk, it does not matter if you talk for longer than was suggested.

10 Using PowerPoint slides is a good idea as you can then read all the points on the slides instead of having to use notes on paper.

11 An impromptu presentation (i.e. one where you have no time to think about it) will probably be better than one you have prepared in advance.

12 It's a good idea to choose one or two people in the audience and then talk to and look at them.

2 Organizing a presentation according to its purpose

Organization is as important in oral presentations as it is in written work. Without organization, your audience will struggle to follow your ideas and you will find it difficult to achieve your purpose. All good presentations have a logical structure. However, as with written work, this structure is not exactly the same for every presentation: it is related to the presentation's aim.

2a Work in pairs. Discuss what different aims your academic presentations may have. Write notes below.

Presentation aims
to present problems and solutions

2b How might the different aims require a different presentation structure?

2c A group of students gave different individual presentations on aspects of wind energy. Each presentation had a particular purpose:

1 To discuss solutions to the problem of wind turbine noise

2 To describe the wind power generation process

3 To assess different viewpoints on the effectiveness of domestic wind turbines

4 To give arguments for and against wind energy.

Work in pairs and predict some information which might have been included in their presentations.

2d Look at the presentation structures the students followed (a–d) and match them with purposes 1–4 in 2c.

a • Introduction
  • Define wind energy
  • Position of wind turbines
  • Rotation of turbine
  • Rotation of shaft
  • Generator produces current
  • Current stored and distributed
  • Conclusion

b • Introduction
  • Define wind energy
  • Advantage 1: harmless, no waste
  • Advantage 2: cost
  • Advantage 3: renewable
  • Disadvantage 1: damage to countryside
  • Disadvantage 2: often out of use
  • Disadvantage 3: not proven long-term
  • Disadvantage 4: not sufficient to meet all power needs
  • Conclusion

c • Introduction
  • Define wind turbine
  • Viewpoint 1: turbine manufacturers
  • Viewpoint 2: government (grants available for alternative energy use)
  • Viewpoint 3: environmental groups
  • Viewpoint 4: turbine users
  • Viewpoint 5: renewable technology expert
  • Conclusion

d • Introduction
  • Define wind turbine
  • Present problem of turbine noise
  • Sources of noise
  • Complaints about noise from public
  • Industry reaction to noise
  • Solution 1: reassess turbine placement (planned projects)
  • Solution 2: technological improvements in design
  • Solution 3: technological improvements in existing turbines (e.g. noise damping)
  • Conclusion

3.10

2e Listen to a student giving one of the presentations above. Which presentation is it?

2f Listen again. Make notes on the information the speaker includes to support their points.

Supporting information

2g Compare your notes with a partner.

2h How effective is the presentation in achieving its purpose? How does the structure help to do this?

> The first step in organizing your presentation successfully is to have a clear idea of what you want to achieve. In some cases your tutor will give you a presentation title. In this case, it is essential to analyze the title carefully so you understand what is expected of you. Remember the four steps you looked at when analyzing written titles in Unit 1 Part E:
> • What is the precise meaning of all of the main terms used in the title?
> • What are the assumptions behind the title?
> • What do the instruction words in the title mean?
> • How many parts are there to the title, and therefore to the essay?
>
> You should then decide which structure is best to achieve the aim of your presentation.

2i Work in pairs. Your tutor has asked you to give a presentation which answers the question: *How can we reduce the impact of household waste on the environment?* Which of the following structures might be suitable in addressing this title? Why?

   a Advantages/disadvantages

   b Describing a process

   c Problem/solution

2j For the presentation question in 2i you have made the mind map below. Work in pairs and discuss these questions.

   1 How might the ideas in the mind map fit in to the presentation structure?

   2 From the research you have done so far, is there anything you would add to the mind map? If so, where in the presentation structure would it belong?

   3 Number the ideas to show the order you would present them in.

2k Listen to a student giving the presentation they planned using the ideas from the mind map. Check your answers to 2j, question 3.

3.11

2l Check your answers with a partner. Do you agree on the same order?

2m Listen again and write notes on the main points of the presentation in the table below.

Notes

2n Work in small groups and discuss how effective the presentation is in achieving its aim. Identify how the organization of the presentation increases effectiveness.

2o Work in small groups. Choose one of these presentation titles. Choose carefully – you should be familiar with the topic!

- A comparison of laptop and desktop computers
- The advantages and/or disadvantages of international study in the UK
- The life cycle of a butterfly
- A history of the Olympic Games
- Sodium chloride and its chemical structure
- Problems and solutions in bridge design
- DNA – a description

2p Use a mind map to brainstorm some ideas for this presentation.

2q Decide which structure(s) would be the most logical for your ideas.

2r Organize your ideas according to your chosen structure using this table.

Main point	Supporting points

2s Give your presentation using the structure you chose.

3 Using visual aids in your presentation

3a Work in pairs. Complete the first column of the table below with as many kinds of visual aids as you can think of.

Visual aid	Advantages	Disadvantages
a real object	• makes point or example very clear • makes presentation more visually appealing	• could be difficult to obtain and transport • size might not be suitable

3b Work in pairs. Discuss the advantages and disadvantages of each kind of visual aid. Complete the second and third columns of the table.

3c Work in small groups. Look at the visual aids on p.119 and discuss the advantages and disadvantages of each one.

3d Put them in order of effectiveness in terms of the amount of information they can convey.

	Visual aid	Reason(s)
1		
2		
3		
4		
5		

Example 1 – graph

Example 2 – graphic/diagram

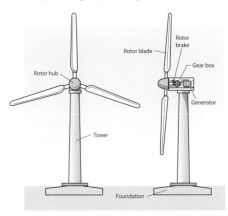

Example 3 – slide with bullet points

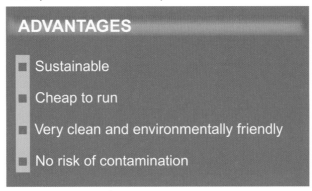

Example 4 – picture

Example 5 – text on a slide

There are a number of disadvantages in this system of generating energy. The most obvious is that the turbines themselves are an eye-sore and often spoil areas of natural beauty. Another is that they produce relatively little energy. Finally …

3e Present the order of effectiveness you chose in 3d to the rest of the class.

4   Designing appropriate visual aids

4a   Work in groups. Look back at the presentation you planned in 2o–2s. Discuss these questions.

1   What visual aid(s) might be used to support the presentation?

2   Is any special equipment/material needed?

4b   Each group member should choose one of the points you planned to present in 2o and design a visual aid to help communicate that point. Design a rough example of a visual aid you might use.

4c   Work in pairs. Answer these questions about your visual aid.

1   Why did you select this visual aid?

2   What decisions did you make in designing the visual aid?

3   How might this visual aid be used in your presentation?

> **UNIT TASK** **Packaging and waste**

In this unit task, you will prepare and give a brief presentation on *The advantages and disadvantages of plastic bags*.

a Work in groups of three or four and choose from one of these two thesis statements.

    1 The advantages of using plastic bags outweigh the disadvantages.

    2 The disadvantages of using plastic bags are so great that we must prevent their use.

b In your group, make a mind map summarizing the research you have done on the topic.

c Structure your presentation. You may like to use a table such as the one in 2r to plan your structure.

d Decide what needs to be done, and how you will complete these tasks. You can allocate tasks to individuals, but be careful to balance the work as evenly as possible and to work together as much as you can. Presentations planned individually and then patched together are rarely effective!

e Give your presentation.

f As you listen to other groups give their presentations, make notes of anything you hadn't included in your own presentation. This will be useful when you are working on the final *Packaging and waste* written task in Part E.

Go to the checklist on p.178. Look again at the tips relating to Unit 3 Parts A–C and tick (✓) those you have used in your studies. Read the tips relating to Unit 3 Part D.

Reporting in writing

By the end of Part E you will be able to:

- create thesis statements
- identify different essay structures
- develop a topic sentence
- develop ideas in writing.

1 Creating thesis statements

1a Work in pairs. Use these four questions from Unit 1 Part E, section 3 to discuss the essay titles (a–d) below.

- What is the precise meaning of all the main terms used in the title?
- What are the assumptions behind the title?
- What do the instruction words in the title mean?
- How many parts are there to the title?

  a Identify and explain the various methods of reducing the effects of global warming.

  b Compare the role of social networking with other methods of forming communities, with reference to the UK.

  c The dangers of nuclear energy are well known. However, advocates insist that using nuclear energy is key to reducing our reliance on fossil fuels. Discuss.

  d Explain what is meant by the *digital divide* and analyze its impact in developing countries.

1b Think about the number of parts for each title from 1a (a–d). What information would you include in an introduction for each essay? Write notes below.

Example
Essay a:

- *What global warming is*
- *Why it needs to be reduced*
- *That there is more than one way to reduce global warming (give examples)*
- *That each method works differently*

Notes

An *introduction* moves from general to more specific topic information. One of the more specific parts of an introduction is known as a *thesis statement*. A thesis statement makes a kind of claim. A thesis statement should

- be specific
- be clear
- tell the reader what to expect from your essay.

A thesis statement may also include sub-topics which will be discussed in the main body of the essay.

To help you write a clear thesis statement, you should include information from the question.

Example
Thesis statement, essay a:

> *With the increase in the number of effects of global warming have come various methods for reducing its consequences; for example, using more nuclear energy, recycling products, and using more energy-efficient products. These varying approaches function in different ways, some being more effective and easier to implement than others.*

1c Work in pairs or small groups. Using the information you noted in 1b, write thesis statements for the essay titles b–d in 1a.

1d Use this checklist to help you decide if your thesis statements are clear.

- Is it specific?
- Will the reader know what information will be included in my essay?
- Does it include information from the question?

2 Identifying different essay structures

2a Each type of essay may be written with a different overall structure. Look again at the essay questions in 1a. Write each essay question (a–d) into the most appropriate space in the second column in the table below. Ignore the third column of the table for now.

Essay type	Essay question	Type number
Advantage/ disadvantage		
Compare/contrast	*b*	*4*
Cause/effect		
Problem/solution		

2b Study the essay structure diagram types below. Which structure type (1–4) best matches each essay type in 2a? Write your answers in the table.

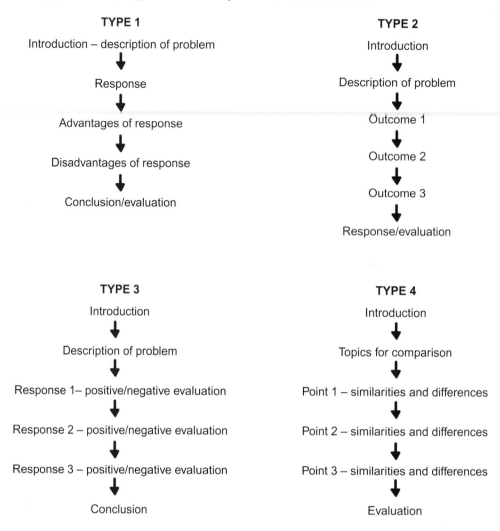

TYPE 1

Introduction – description of problem
↓
Response
↓
Advantages of response
↓
Disadvantages of response
↓
Conclusion/evaluation

TYPE 2

Introduction
↓
Description of problem
↓
Outcome 1
↓
Outcome 2
↓
Outcome 3
↓
Response/evaluation

TYPE 3

Introduction
↓
Description of problem
↓
Response 1– positive/negative evaluation
↓
Response 2 – positive/negative evaluation
↓
Response 3 – positive/negative evaluation
↓
Conclusion

TYPE 4

Introduction
↓
Topics for comparison
↓
Point 1 – similarities and differences
↓
Point 2 – similarities and differences
↓
Point 3 – similarities and differences
↓
Evaluation

3   Developing a topic sentence

A topic sentence is frequently used at the beginning of a paragraph and indicates the idea (or topic) of the paragraph. Topic sentences are often developed by adding a focus. The focus offers more detailed information about how the topic will be developed.

Example

Topic: *People can avoid problems with internet security.*

This tells you the paragraph is about avoiding problems with internet security.

Focus: *People need to take simple precautions.*

This tells us the paragraph will focus on simple precautions people can take.

Topic sentence: *People can avoid problems with internet security by taking a few simple precautions.*

3a Identify the topic and focus in these sentences:

- Another disadvantage is that children without access to information online have educational disadvantages compared to those who do.
- While it is clear that a digital divide exists between the developed and developing nations, there is also a digital divide within nations as well.
- There are other serious effects of the digital divide, in particular the isolating effect of lack of access to IT among the elderly.
- A cheap computer, designed for use in schools in developing nations, has been developed by the One Laptop Per Child project.
- Even though much has been written about the causes of the digital divide in recent years, relatively little attention has been paid to its long-term effects.

3b Think of some appropriate topic sentences for these ideas on internet security.

1

Topic sentence:

According to Evans (2001), when an email is sent or a browser is used to get access to a website, the chances of communication being intercepted among the millions of other similar communications travelling in cyberspace are infinitesimal. The privacy risks begin when an email passes through a node on its way to its destination or is sitting on a server, because both can be hacked into by malicious or criminal people. When you access a website, the server which carries your request will be logged and identified. In other words, your personal information is not really well protected: it can be stolen easily. This information may then be used for illegal purposes.

2

Topic sentence:

As pointed out by Ryrie (2002), access to an email can be achieved by anyone with the right level of network administration access to any server it resides in. Perhaps the only way to reduce security risks is to encrypt the email, i.e. add passwords to the computer system.

3

Topic sentence:

Ferington (2003) warns that hackers keep trying different combinations of characters in the hope of hitting upon a password that works. Making a correct guess is not impossible, as is evident in the incident reported by Schmidt (1999). In August 1999 even Microsoft itself had to shut down its own free Hotmail service because of hackers' attacks. In this instance the hackers created websites that allowed anyone unrestricted access to any Hotmail account. As a result, the password protection was destroyed. This shows that encryption is not really a totally effective method of solving the problem.

4 Developing ideas in writing

> Once you have established the main topic of each paragraph, you then need to develop the idea in some way. Some suggestions to help you develop your ideas are:
> - Explain an advantage/disadvantage
> - Examine effects and consequences
> - Compare and contrast features
> - Evaluate/analyze a response

4a Work in three groups. Read the text your tutor allocates to you and answer the questions.

A

The demographics of those using social networks have not changed significantly in recent years. One study (Perceval, 2010) shows that, in 2009, the rate of people using social networks for those aged 15 and over was 86 per cent. This is somewhat similar to the 2007 rate of 84 per cent but considerably higher than the 2005 rate of 54 per cent. These figures represent an environment where people have better access to broadband Internet and cheaper computers. Furthermore, rates of use of social networks for 2009 showed no significant sex difference in the proportion of the population aged 15 and over (males 87 per cent and females 85 per cent). This was also the case in 2007. In 2005, however, the rate for males was significantly higher than the rate for females. Among children aged 5–14, there was no significant difference by sex or age. Among those aged 15 and over in 2009, the number of people using social networks regularly was lowest in the 55–64 years age group (36 per cent), followed, perhaps surprisingly, by the 65–74 years age group.

1 How has this idea been developed? Choose from the four bullet points above.

2 What phrases does the writer use to indicate a change?

3 What phrases does the writer use to indicate a similarity?

4 What could the topic/focus of the next paragraph be?

B

It has been argued that the use of social networks may lead to health problems. Scientists identify several reasons for this. Firstly, the rise in the amount of time people are spending online, particularly for young people, may contribute to changes in the brains of young users (Greenfield, 2009). These changes have been linked to short attention spans and even increased incidences of autism. Although the exact causes of autism have not been established, there is growing concern (Mail, 2009) that an increased prevalence of people spending time in computer relationships may be a factor in autism in young children. Secondly, spending time in front of screens may also carry a high risk that repeated exposure could re-wire the brain. Greenfield (2009) argues that spending large amounts of time on online social network may encourage instant gratification and make young people more self-centred.

1 How has this idea been developed? Choose from the four bullet points above.

2 How does the writer signal each new point?

3 What phrases does the writer use to indicate a cause–effect relationship?

4 How could you develop the argument in the next paragraph?

C

Social networking sites have opened up a number of new possibilities in education. One such capability is blogging. Trevor (2007) states that the interactivity of a blog is a good example of how traditional web pages have developed to facilitate and promote communication. Schools, colleges and universities are finding ways of turning blogs into learning aids, using them to create projects, offer feedback, post assignments and evaluate class progress. Moreover, as Griffin (2010) points out, the use of a blog can add a social, cultural and collaborative dimension to learning.

However, despite the almost overwhelming enthusiasm for the use of blogs and blogging for educational purposes, there has been a growing feeling of discontent. Barnes (2006) points out that one of the criticisms of blogs, especially student blogs, is that many people write about nothing but trivia. Blogs can too quickly become a focus of one's ego. Moreover, some of the benefits of blogs may be lost. Although blogging provides learners with a real-life audience outside the classroom, there is still a danger that the audience will be the teacher and other students – much like a classroom. There is also a risk that as soon as topics are given in the context of schoolwork or coursework, they automatically lose a level of authenticity.

1 How has this idea been developed? Choose from the four bullet points on p.126.

2 What phrases does the writer use to indicate the development of the idea?

3 How does the writer signal a change in the argument?

4 How could you develop this idea further?

4b Work in a group with students who read the other texts and discuss these questions.

1 How do the writers develop their ideas?

2 How do the writers organize their ideas?

3 Write examples of linking language and what they are used to indicate in this table.

Linking word(s) or expression(s)	Used to indicate …
This is somewhat similar to …	similarity

4c You are going to develop your own paragraph on 'Packaging and waste' based on the text in Unit 3 Part B, Unit task.

1 Make a mind map or list to brainstorm ideas on the topic.

2 From your mind map, choose one idea to develop as a paragraph.

3 Express this idea as a topic sentence.

4 Think about how you will develop this idea. What structure will you use? What information do you need to support the topic sentence?

5 Write your paragraph. Think about how you can link and signal your ideas clearly.

4d Compare your paragraph with a partner. Can you identify the structure?

> **UNIT TASK** **Packaging and waste**

Using the ideas from the texts you have read and the ideas presented by other groups in Part D of this Unit, write a formal problem–solution essay with this title:

'In 2008, an estimated 10.7 million tonnes of packaging waste was disposed of in the UK. (Department of Environment, Food and Rural Affairs, 2008). If this continues, the environmental impact could be catastrophic.'

Discuss the problems associated with disposing of large amounts of waste, then identify different ways of reducing the amount of waste people produce. In your essay, you should refer to a number of sources and can include your own ideas on this topic. Try to provide a list of references at the end. The essay should be approximately 750 words.

a Write an essay plan below.

Essay plan for: Problems of waste

b Work in small groups and answer these questions about your essay plans.

1 Why have you selected these points? How are they relevant? Do you have enough (reliable) support?

2 Why have you selected this structure? Is it clear and logical?

c Make any necessary modifications to your plan and then write your essay.

 Go to the checklist on p.178. Look again at the tips relating to Unit 3 Parts A–D and tick (✓) those you have used in your studies. Read the tips relating to Unit 3 Part E.

Unit 4 Health issues

Unit overview

Part	This part will help you to …	By improving your ability to …
A	**Listen critically**	• understand different types of signposting • understand the speaker's purpose • understand the speaker's attitude to the information.
B	**Understand, compare and summarize texts**	• understand ways to improve your reading • read to compare information • write effective summaries.
C	**Find and record relevant information**	• keep detailed records • record correct bibliographic information • keep a detailed scientific logbook • establish the relevance of abstracts • identify common features of abstracts • use an abstract for research.
D	**Deliver a pair presentation**	• define a purpose for a presentation • be aware of your audience • give effective pair presentations • plan and produce a poster.
E	**Create a piece of academic writing**	• write an introduction • write a conclusion • review your written work.

Understanding spoken information

By the end of Part A you will be able to:

- understand different types of signposting
- understand the speaker's purpose
- understand the speaker's attitude to the information.

1 Different types of signposting

In Unit 3, you were briefly introduced to signposting language, which can help you predict and follow the connections between ideas in lectures and also understand the speaker's stance on the topic.

Signposting language can be particularly useful in longer lectures, where it can be quite easy to get lost because of the amount of subject information. However, rather than panic if this happens, listen out for the signposts which will bring you back onto the correct 'path'. You should then be able to refocus and resume your note-taking.

You are going to add to some of the signposting expressions you studied in Unit 3. The table below contains several examples of commonly used signposting language.

1a Work in pairs. Decide where each expression belongs in the table below (more than one answer is possible in many cases).

Another point worth noting is …	~~As for …~~	At the same time …
Furthermore …	However …	In addition …
In contrast …	Moving now to …	Secondly …
Therefore …	With regard to …	So …

Signposting expressions	
Expressions to change topic (tell you what the speaker will talk about next)	*Let's turn now to …* *My next topic is …*
Contrasting expressions (introduce an opposing idea within a topic)	*But …*
Connecting expressions (show agreement between ideas / build on an existing idea)	*Also …*
Focusing expressions (direct attention to a particular topic)	*As for …*

1b You are going to hear an extract from a lecture about young people's health. Work in small groups. Discuss these questions.

1 How do you define 'health'?

2 How seriously do young people consider their health?

3 Is there a connection between being healthy and being attractive?

4.1

1c Listen to the extract from the lecture. Write notes on the information relevant to questions 1–3 in 1b.

Part 1: Notes
1
2
3

1d Check your answers with a partner. How do the speaker's points compare with your own answers to questions 1–3 in 1b?

1e Listen again. As you listen, pay attention to the signposting. Tick (✓) the signposting expressions you hear.

Firstly …	Now …	In contrast …	Secondly …
As for …	However …	My next topic is …	Turning now to …
But rather …	Also …		

1f Work in small groups. Discuss some of the factors which affect young people's health and how these can be addressed. Write notes on your ideas in the second column below.

Young people	Group ideas	Lecture
Factors which affect health 1 Exercise 2 Eating habits 3 Medical condition 4 Sleep		
Suggestions for improving health 1 Government controls 2 Education 3 Eating habits 4 Exercise 5 Sleep		

4.2

1g Listen to the next extract from the lecture and write notes in the third column of the table in 1f. Remember, if you get lost, listen out for the next signposting expression to signal order or a change in topic and start to make notes again on that topic.

1h Work in groups. Answer these questions.

1   How similar were the ideas in the lecture to your own?

2   Do you agree with the lecturer's opinion?

2   Signposting – the speaker's purpose

4.3

2a Listen to two short extracts from a lecture. For each version of the talk, decide what part of the lecture the extract is from. Make brief notes of your answers below.

Extract 1
Extract 2

2b In which extract was it easier to understand what the speaker was doing? Why?

> Some signposting expressions can be used to tell you what the speaker is *doing* at a certain point. Understanding the speaker's purpose in this way can help you listen more critically to the content of the talk.

4.4

2c Listen to three short extracts from a lecture. Tick (✓) the expressions (a–q) you hear.

1 Concluding a speech	a To conclude
2 Making a hypothesis	b To go off topic for a moment
	c I hypothesize that
3 Showing doubt	d I will pause here at this point to consider
	e I predict that
4 Agreeing with something	f Looking back at the main points again
5 Digressing	g I will illustrate this
	h I would doubt that
6 Reviewing what has already been said	i To pause for a moment
	j To give an example
7 Making a prediction	k I guess that
8 Giving an example	l In summary
	m To make a prediction
	n To sum up
	o In support of this idea
	p To digress
	q So, to review

2d The first column of the table in 2c contains some common things that a speaker can do while giving a talk. Match them with the expressions in the second column. One of the expressions can be used more than once.

3   Signposting – the speaker's attitude to the information

> Each speaker will have their own feelings about the subject content that they present in a talk. Signposting can give you clues about the speaker's opinions on the topic, which in turn can help you listen critically and develop your own ideas on the subject by thinking about how far you agree/disagree with the speaker.
>
> For example, in the first of the two statements below, the speaker is sure that mobile phones are bad for your health, but in the second statement, there's an element of doubt.
> * *Undoubtedly, mobile phones are bad for your health.*
> * *It is possible that mobile phones are bad for your health.*

3a   The table below contains three types of signposting, each of which reflects the speaker's opinion. Work in small groups. Write each item in the most appropriate section of the table (some may be used for more than one purpose).

Definitely …	I agree …	I would hope that …
It is a sad fact that …	It is obvious that …	It seems doubtful that …
It seems likely that …	… might …	Perhaps …
Undoubtedly …	Unfortunately …	Actually …

Signposting expressions	
Hedging expressions (suggest that the speaker is not totally certain if a statement is true or not)	*It is possible that …* *… may …*
Certainty expressions (the speaker is certain that a statement is true)	*In fact …* *It is clear that …*
Attitude expressions (show the speaker's personal feelings about the subject)	*Surprisingly …* *I find it interesting that …*

3b   Add some of your own expressions to the table.

3c   You are writing an essay with the title *To what extent can human longevity be controlled by science?* Work in pairs. Identify the key terms in the title and discuss their meaning.

3d Work in pairs. You are going to listen to a lecture about human lifespan. Before you listen, discuss what factors are mainly responsible for human longevity.

3e Listen to two extracts from a lecture about human longevity and write notes below.

4.5

Extract 1

Extract 2

3f Use your notes to help you answer these questions.

Extract 1
1 Does the speaker think the so-called 'elixir of life' is likely to be discovered?
2 How certain is the speaker that a gene for longevity does not exist?
3 What does the speaker think is the most likely explanation for a long lifespan? How does this compare with your own opinion?

Extract 2
4 Is the speaker certain that science cannot guarantee longevity?
5 What does the speaker believe about the reasons for Okinawan longevity?
6 What is the speaker's opinion about breast cancer statistics in Okinawa?

3g Look at the listening transcript in **Appendix 7**. Circle the signposting expressions which show hedging, certainty and attitude and add any new ones to the table in 3a.

3h Work in pairs. You are going to listen to a lecture given by a business consultant about how to manage stress at work. Before you listen, try to predict which of the following topics will be included in the talk.

Discussion of whether stress is real or not
Seriousness of problem
Causes
Effects on employee
The link between stress and smoking

Plan for managers to reduce stress
Awareness of issues
Educating the workforce
Positive effects of meditation and yoga
Stress management programmes

3i Listen to the lecture. Check your answers to 3h.

4.6

3j Listen again and add as much extra information as you can to the notes on p.135.

Notes on stress at work

Seriousness of problem

Causes

Effects on employee

Plan for managers to reduce stress

Awareness of issues

Educating the workforce

Stress management programmes

3k Look over your notes in 3j again. Which points that the speaker made do you agree/disagree with, and why?

3l Work in groups. Use your notes to help you discuss the best way of tackling workplace stress. Share your recommendations with the rest of the class.

➤ UNIT TASK   Health expectancy

The Unit 4 task is about health expectancy. At the end of each part, you will be asked to complete a stage of the task as follows:

Part A: Listen to an introduction on the topic.

Part B: Read two texts about it.

Part C: Do some further research for relevant material.

Part D: Give a short presentation on the topic.

Part E: Write an essay with one of these titles:

Examine the factors that contribute to increased health expectancy.

or

Compare the health expectancy situation in two countries of your choice.

In this first unit task, you will listen to an introduction to the subject.

a   Work in pairs. Discuss what you think the differences are between life and health expectancy. Write your ideas below.

Life expectancy – definition	Health expectancy – definition

b   Make a list of possible factors which might affect health expectancy.

Factors which might affect health expectancy

c   Listen to a lecture about health expectancy. Health expectancy is related to life expectancy, though there are some important differences. Make complete notes on definitions and relevant factors in your notes above.

4.7

d   Compare your notes with a partner to check you got all the key points. You will need these notes for the final task of this unit.

Go to the checklist on p.179 and read the tips relating to Unit 4 Part A.

Understanding written information

By the end of Part B you will be able to:

- understand ways to improve your reading
- read to compare information
- write effective summaries.

1 Ways to improve your reading

1a Look at this advice about reading at college and university. Tick (✓) the three pieces of advice you think are the most useful.

1 Manage your time – you will be expected to read a lot so make time during the week when you can dedicate yourself to your reading. Make sure it is a time when you are not hungry or tired.

2 Think about how your reading helps you with your studies. What information are you looking for? Where are you most likely to find it?

3 Choose an appropriate reading strategy. Do you scan texts quickly for specific information? Do you read other parts more carefully to get a deeper understanding?

4 You don't have to read every word of every text. Use features of a text to guide you to the parts you need (chapters, pages, paragraphs, pictures, headings, etc.).

5 When looking for information to support your ideas, scan the text and, if it's your own copy, underline or highlight the parts that may be useful. This makes it easier to find later on.

6 Reread difficult parts. Academic writing is aimed at a very specific audience. Don't worry if you don't understand everything. That is why you are learning. You will improve with practice.

7 Every time you use your reading in your assignments, reference it. Don't be afraid of using lots of sources in your work.

1b Compare the three pieces of advice you ticked with a partner. Did you agree? Can you think of any more advice to add to the list?

2 Reading to compare information

2a You have been given the assignment task *Compare and contrast health expectancy in two developed countries*. Work in pairs. Discuss the definition of *developed countries*. Then brainstorm the kind of information you should look for.

2b You have found information on two countries: New Zealand and the UK. Before you read, discuss these questions as a class.

1 What do you already know about health expectancy?

2 How might health expectancy compare between New Zealand and the UK?

3 What factors may cause any differences?

4 Do you think there will be any differences between males and females?

2c Look at this information relating to health expectancy in New Zealand and the UK. Work in pairs. What similarities and differences are there? In what way are they significant? Write notes below.

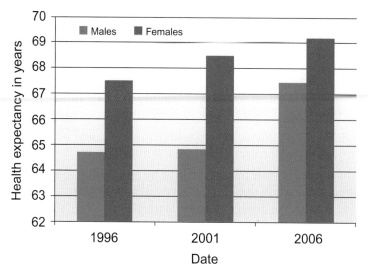

Figure 1: Health expectancy at birth by gender, 1996, 2001 and 2006 (New Zealand Ministry of Health, 2010)

Table 1: Health expectancy at birth by country and sex, 2000–2002, 2004–2006 in the United Kingdom

Country	Male Healthy Life Expectancy		Female Healthy Life Expectancy	
	2000–2002	2004–2006	2000–2002	2004–2006
United Kingdom	66.8	68.2	69.9	70.4
Great Britain	66.8	68.2	69.9	70.5
England	67.1	68.5	70.1	70.7
Wales	65.5	66.7	69.4	68.9
Scotland	65.3	66.5	68.6	69.6
Northern Ireland	65.1	66.9	67.2	68.8

Notes

2d These two texts provide information on health expectancy in New Zealand and the UK. As you read the texts, add any relevant ideas to the notes you made in 2c.

The Health Expectancy Situation in New Zealand

Good physical health is very closely related to a person's overall well-being, with poor health making it much more difficult to enjoy a rewarding and happy life. There are two main elements to good health: longevity, or lifespan, and the overall quality of life. On the whole, people desire both that they will live a long life, but also a life free from serious illness, disease or disability. Although many people recognize that they may become dependent on the support of others at some time in their life, it is considered important that this dependency is minimized. However, a number of people will require support offered by families, the government or healthcare systems in order to function fully in society. Access to this support is also understood to contribute to a sense of contentment and overall well-being. For people with either physical or mental illness or injury, there are significant obstacles to participating fully in the workforce or education, which has consequences for their ability to earn a satisfactory living later in life, join in with community events or even simply enjoy leisure activities with friends or family.

The factors which affect (and are in turn affected by) health status include personal behaviour and attitudes, the social environment, the physical surroundings in which people live, and even genetic predispositions to certain illnesses. Greater attention is now being paid to the relationship between health, well-being and socio-economic status, as it becomes evident that poor health is likely to emerge from lack of education, low income, and poor accommodation.

Indicators

This article will focus on six indicators of health, including both physical health and overall well-being, which reveal both the nation's present situation and probable future trends. These indicators include: life expectancy, health expectancy (disability-free life expectancy allowing a life lived independently of support), suicide rate, obesity, potentially dangerous consumption of alcohol, and smoking cigarettes. Life and health expectancy as well as suicide give a picture of the current state of national health, while obesity rates and consumption levels of tobacco and alcoholic drinks are strong indicators of future health trends.

Life and health expectancy are commonly accepted measures of a population's general physical health and rates of mortality, while suicide provides a picture of the nation's mental health situation, from which a sense of the general social well-being can be judged. The suicide rate measures both national suicide rate as well as providing details of the rate among different social subgroups. Recent years have seen a fall in the New Zealand suicide rate overall, although with a higher rate of suicide by young people than many other OECD countries.

The indicators of future health have a widely acknowledged predictive power, with clear links between smoking and various forms of respiratory and cardiovascular illness, low birth-weight, as well as a variety of cancers. In a similar way, obesity is strongly linked to stroke, type 2 diabetes, some cancers and heart attacks. Alcohol is commonly consumed throughout New Zealand, though most people tend to consume it in moderate amounts. Potentially dangerous drinking is classified as a pattern of alcohol consumption that risks the individual's future health, both physical and mental, even though these effects have yet to emerge. Alcohol's secondary effects on health include injury or death in accidents or violence.

Health expectancy in the present study

Health expectancy as a measure of population health covers both physical health and well-being, which are often popularly described together as the quantity and quality of life. The health expectancy situation of the nation as a whole may improve due to shifting trends in lifestyle, improvements in medical care and heightened socio-economic conditions. This study takes health expectancy to be the number of years that an individual may expect to live in good health, where good health is understood to be living independently, without any functional disabilities that would need help from a complex assistive device or another person. This is known as ILE, or Independent Life Expectancy but will be referred to in this report simply as 'health expectancy'.

This measure was calculated from 1996, 2001, and 2006 national disability surveys. In 2006, the estimated health expectancy at birth stood at 67.4 years for New Zealand males and slightly higher, at 69.2 years, for females. The gender gap between health expectancy estimates in 2006 (1.8 years) has decreased since 2001, when it was 3.6 years. Overall, the average health expectancy for the entire New Zealand population has improved since 1996.

Differences among ethnic groups

Health expectancy for Maori was arrived at in the same way as for the New Zealand population as a whole. In 2006, Maori males had health expectancy at birth of 62 years, while female Maoris could expect 64.2 years of healthy life. Maori communities tended to show a lower health expectancy than other New Zealanders. In 2006, the health expectancy gap between Maori and non-Maori populations stood at 6.8 years for males, and 6.2 years for females.

Adapted from: Ministry of Social Development. (2010). *Social Report 2010*. Wellington: New Zealand Ministry of Social Development.

B

Health Expectancy in The United Kingdom

Definitions

Life expectancy has for a long time been the most common measure of the statistical health of a population. Life expectancy is simply the estimate of lifespan at birth for an individual or representative population. Increasingly, however, health expectancy is used to give a sense of the proportion of that life which will be spent in a state of so-called 'good' health. In the present paper, health expectancy will be taken to mean Healthy Life Expectancy (HLE), the percentage of lifespan that an individual is expected to remain free from serious disability or disease which limits their ability to perform physical or social functions independently. It should be noted that this estimate is not an accurate reflection of actual expected good health for any single individual, as the national health statistics are likely to change during the course of an individual's lifetime due to advances in medical care and changes in the population due to immigration or economic improvements.

Sources of data for the health expectancy estimates

The UK data presented here is primarily taken from surveys conducted for the Office for National Statistics (ONS). These include the General Household Survey in Great Britain, and the Continuous Household Survey in Northern Ireland.

The current health expectancy situation in The United Kingdom

In the UK in 2006, the average male health expectancy was 68.2 years at birth. Males reaching the age of 65 in 2006 could, on average, look forward to another 12.8 years in good health. UK females had health expectancy of 70.4 years at birth and 14.5 years at age 65 (Smith et al., 2008, p.77).

On average, health expectancy improved slightly for UK residents in the period from 1981 to 2007 (ONS, 2010). This is in line with modest health expectancy advances in other OECD countries (Robine et al., 2005). The overall causes of this improvement can be ascribed to individual and societal factors. On an individual level, the last two decades have seen a boom in health related fashions, including physical exercise, an increased interest in healthy eating and personal care, and a downward trend in risky behaviours such as smoking and excessive consumption of alcohol.

At a societal level, the improvement in health expectancy emerges from improvements in medical technology and access. Several illnesses which are commonly associated with ageing, such as heart disease and stroke, are now tackled with a combination of better clinical care and greater public awareness of prevention than in previous decades. UK residents on average have a heightened awareness of the risks of smoking, and the period 1993 to 2006 has seen a fall in the number of smokers (NHSIC, 2008, pp.4–5). The

United Kingdom enjoyed a period of wealth and economic growth from the mid-1990s until 2008, which is also likely to have contributed to the higher health expectancy figures. The link between socio-economic status and lifetime health has been clearly shown in studies throughout the world, and The United Kingdom is no exception (see, for instance, White and Edgar, 2010). The benefits of this prosperity have shown themselves in better education and housing, and shifting public appetites for healthier lifestyles.

Ethnic and regional differences

Health expectancy averages for the entire country should not be depended upon to provide a clear picture of the health status of different subgroups within the nation, as there tend to be considerable variations between populations from different ethnic backgrounds, and a somewhat smaller variation between England and other regions. Residents in England enjoy much better health expectancies overall than in the other nations of the UK (Smith et al., 2008, p.78).

UK residents of Anglo-Saxon or European heritage tend to enjoy both greater life and health expectancy than ethnic minorities with origins in South Asia (Chandola, 2001). These differences can be attributed to a range of factors, though Chandola argues that poorer health among British South Asians results from lower socio-economic status and related effects of living in poorer local areas. However, it should be noted that the health expectancy of ethnic minorities in the UK needs more research, as these members of the community tend to be underrepresented in surveys.

Predicted future trends

In the current period the health status of the United Kingdom is comparable to that of other OECD nations and counterparts in the EU. However, obesity levels, which declined throughout the early 1990s, have been rising swiftly since the mid 1990s (NHSIC, 2008, p.4). This does not equate to an immediate decline in health expectancy, as the negative physical and psychological impacts of morbid obesity take years to emerge across the population as a whole. It is to be expected that, if current trends in obesity continue, the gains made in other areas of health may be reduced within the next two decades. This prediction, however, does not account for the fact that medical advances in the coming years may push health expectancy up despite risk behaviours such as poor diet or overconsumption. Health expectancy differences between subgroups of the population are likely to become more apparent.

References

Chandola, T. (2001). Ethnic and class differences in health in relation to British South Asians: using the new National Statistics Socio-Economic Classification. *Social Science & Medicine, 52*(8), 1285–1296.

Office for National Statistics. (2010). Health Expectancy: living longer in poorer health. Retrieved from http://www.statistics.gov.uk/cci/nugget.asp?id=934

Robine, J., Jagger, C., Clavel, A., and Romieu, I. (2005). *Disability-Free Life Expectancy (DFLE) in EU Countries from 1991 to 2003*. Montpellier: EHEMU.

Smith, M., Edgar, G., and Groom, G. (2008). Health expectancies in the United Kingdom, 2004–06. *Health Statistics Quarterly, 37,* 77–80.

The NHS Information Centre. (2008). *Health survey for England 2006: latest trends.* London: Office for National Statistics.

White, C., and Edgar, G. (2010). Inequalities in healthy life expectancy by social class and area type: England, 2001–03. *Health Statistics Quarterly, 45*, 28–56.

2e Compare your notes with a partner.

2f Read these notes on the articles and correct any information that is incorrect, inaccurate or not mentioned.

Health expectancy, New Zealand and the UK

- Health expectancy – the length of time a person may live healthily (physically and mentally). Different from life expectancy.
- No difference between health expectancy now and health expectancy at birth.
- Women have a longer health expectancy – gender is an important difference. Women are more likely to have a poor income and poor housing but live longer.
- In the UK, people of South Asian origin have poorer health expectancies. Health expectancy reflects the relative wealth of different people.
- In New Zealand in 2006, Maoris had the shortest Health Expectancy at birth.
- People in New Zealand live healthier lives than people in the UK.
- Smoking, obesity and alcohol all have an effect on health expectancy.
- Different factors affect health expectancy – social, physical, economical, gender, race.
- Women smoke less and drink less in New Zealand and therefore live longer.
- If you drink red wine, you live longer. Smoking means you will be unhealthy even if you don't die. Obesity causes lung disease and type 2 diabetes.
- Health expectancy for everyone – regardless of race, gender – is rising.

2g Add any further information to your notes from 2c.

3 Writing effective summaries

3a Work in pairs. Discuss whether these statements about summarizing are true (T) or false (F).

1 It is OK to keep words and phrases from the original text so the meaning stays the same.
2 You should always give citations for information from expert sources.
3 Use phrases to introduce ideas into your assignments (e.g. *The study states that* ...).
4 The summary should always reflect your ideas about the text.
5 You should include minor ideas, definitions and detailed examples from a text.
6 Write your summary from your notes and not directly from the text.
7 Clearly indicate that you are summarizing someone else's work.
8 You may include your own ideas and opinions to show you have thought critically about your reading.

3b Work in pairs. Read three summaries of text A in 2d. Discuss which of the summaries you think is the best one.

Summary 1

Health expectancy situation in New Zealand

According to a study by the New Zealand Ministry of Social Development (2010), there is a need for some kind of support – either provided by the state, privately, or by families – for those who are unable to contribute to the workforce. The author notes that the extent of aid an individual will need depends on their socio-economic background. The study addresses six signs of good health (life expectancy, health expectancy, suicide rate, obesity, extreme alcohol consumption and cigarette smoking) and these are divided into two areas: one which reflects the current state of national health (suicide rate, life and health expectancy) and one which projects the future state of the nation (obesity, cigarette smoking).

The study states that health expectancy includes both physical and mental well-being, both of which can be affected by quality of life, race and gender (2006 male life expectancy was 67.4, female 69.2, Maori male 62 and Maori female 64.2).

Surveys measuring Independent Life Expectancy (ILE) (1996, 2001 and 2006) indicated that overall life expectancy in New Zealand has improved, although it is unclear if this is linked to the Maori population. The author suggests that this may be due to better standards of living.

Summary 2

The studies show that health expectancy has risen in New Zealand in the past twenty years. However, the rise in health expectancy was not equal for all sectors of society. According to the studies, women have a longer health expectancy than men (69.2 years and 67.4 years respectively, for example). Moreover, sections of society with lower economic status had shorter health expectancy.

Summary 3

Health and life expectancy are not the same and there are many factors which affect them. The article looks at some of these factors. Health expectancy as a measure of population health covers both physical and mental well-being, which are often popularly described together as the quality of life. The study referred to in the article shows that health expectancy is different for different people. Health expectancy can change if lifestyle changes.

3c Work in small groups. Discuss these questions and make notes of the main points made during the discussion.

1 What similarities and differences do you think there are between your country and New Zealand and the UK in terms of health expectancy?

2 What could be done to raise health expectancy?

3 What effect does economic status seem to have on health expectancy? Why is this?

3d Write a short paragraph of similar length to those in 3b, introducing your discussion in 3c. Use your notes to help you.

 **UNIT TASK** **Health expectancy**

In this unit task, you will research information on one of these titles:

Examine the factors that contribute to increased health expectancy.

or

Compare the health expectancy situation in two countries of your choice.

In this second unit task, you will critically read and take notes on two texts.

a Read each text and take notes about the factors affecting health expectancy. As you read, you should consider these questions:

  1 What similar information do the two sources present?
  2 Are there any differences in the opinions or claims that the authors of the two articles present?
  3 What factors in health expectancy are described in the two reports?
  4 Which of these factors can individuals change, thereby possibly increasing their healthy lifespan?
  5 Which of these factors are outside an individual's control?

b Compare your notes with a partner. Discuss these questions:
  1 Do your notes contain citations and page numbers?
  2 Are your notes brief and efficient?
  3 Are your notes clearly organized?

A Maintaining a healthy lifestyle into old age

Adapted from: Green, C. (2003) *College English Creative Reading (Book 3)*, © Macmillan Publishers.

How do some people achieve a happy and healthy old age, while others die early or end their lives suffering from some kind of serious disease? To some extent the answer is genetic longevity – the tendency to live a long life which a person inherits from his/her mother and father.

There is no doubt that if your grandparents and parents were free of heart disease and cancer you stand a better than average chance of living a long life. But medical scientists agree that genetics cannot, on its 'own', explain why some people live longer than others do. Environmental factors are important, too. Non-genetic considerations include diet (in this context what a person eats rather than a deliberately restricted intake of food), exercise, outlook on life, attitude to change, and temperament.

To take the last point first: evidence supports the claim that a calm temper favours longevity. People who are aggressive, emotional or constantly anxious are at a serious disadvantage. The outcome of a hot temperament is – inevitably – stress, and stress carries with it many problems. The ability to stay calm and to relax is important to health and the achievement of a happy old age. Being relaxed does not contradict the idea of having passionate interests. Indeed, eagerness to pursue chosen subjects is vital for long life. The subject or interest is immaterial: it could be a physical passion such as dancing, a love of music or of books, or simply meeting new people.

One thing is very clear, however: as they get older, people must avoid becoming resistant to change; thinking that the 'old days' were better than 'these days' and complaining about how the world is deteriorating and criticizing the younger generation are sure signs of an early death. Adults who wish to live to a happy old age need to have an enthusiasm for some aspect of life. If they are retired, they should get involved in some new and interesting activity. They should remember this: 'You don't stop doing things because you grow old. You grow old because you stop doing things.' A very true saying.

Now, some people are naturally more physically active than others and are at a considerable advantage compared to their 'couch potato' fellows – lazy, TV-watching people. But their activities should not simply be the result of stress. Some aging exercisers – the person who visits the gym seven times a week, for example – may be displaying a conscious or unconscious anxiety about their health. If they take exercise too seriously it will work against them. It is a myth that only strenuous exercise will lead to fitness. Older individuals who take up intensive athletic activity such as marathon running and competitive squash are usually people who fear declining health.

In fact, it is crucial that physical exercise – as we grow past the young sportsman stage – should be extensive (not causing the heart rate to rise significantly) rather than intensive and, above all, fun to do – something to look forward to. Mature exercisers should not worry if they don't sweat – sweating leads only to weight loss in terms of water and exercise doesn't make you eat more and so get fatter. On the contrary, after an exercise session the appetite is suppressed and the body continues to burn calories for many hours.

As regards intake – substances taken into the body – the long-lived have a generally moderate diet. Extremes of diet are not common – healthy people do not spend a month eating nothing or eating only a particular kind of food. One famous diet, for example, requires people to eat only cabbage soup for a month! A balanced diet which provides carbohydrates, protein, fibre, minerals and vitamins favours longevity and vibrant good health. As well as being balanced, intake should also be regular and modern people have decided that three meals a day should be standard. However, our eating habits are not natural but are rather shaped by our working lives and this has some very undesirable consequences. Most of us are in too much of a hurry to get to work to have a good breakfast – the most important meal of the day since it follows a ten-hour period in which nothing has been eaten or drunk. But equally most of us have plenty of time to enjoy the evening meal – the least important for health!

In fact, eating small, frequent and healthy meals is probably better for us and was almost certainly the way our ancestors ate. Eating between meals is fine provided you don't have the meals! Generally speaking, eating between meals to give yourself a boost is not healthy. This kind of snacking just increases the level of sugar in the blood and gives a very temporary energy increase. Certainly, some kinds of food should be avoided and this includes all the junk foods such as instant noodles, french fries, hamburgers, chips, biscuits, cake and chocolate. These foods are extremely high in calories and too many calories make you fat – to use up the energy you get from eating a small bar of chocolate you would need to walk briskly for about two hours!

Temperament, exercise and diet are not, of course, the only factors involved in achieving good health and longevity – being successful, for example, is a great life-stretcher, and can even override such life-shorteners as obesity, which means being dangerously overweight, and a liking for tobacco. However, success must always be measured in personal terms. So, a carpenter may feel just as successful in his own way as a prize-winning scientist and the shop assistant who finds the job satisfying may be a far happier, and hence healthier, person than the doctor who is not really suited to that profession. Long-lived individuals seem to be more concerned with what they do than who they are.

Most long-lived people are distinguished by a sense of self-discipline. The person who lives long because he/she walks a mile a day does so because he does it every day, as part of an organized existence. A happy existence filled with health-giving laughter. Those who have such self-discipline are able to maintain their healthy habits without giving in to the temptation of laziness: they continue to do exercise even if they feel tired, and avoid overindulging in foods or behaviours which are less healthy.

And so finally to sleep. Many people need between 6 and 8 hours per night but some survive quite happily on far less. In fact, many doctors are more concerned about the negative indications associated with oversleeping: sleeping for longer than 9 hours regularly might well be a sign that an individual is depressed.

Environmental and behavioural factors emerge from a number of studies as important factors in lifelong health, and indeed the promotion of healthy longevity. It seems that the key to a successful old age might not be access to a good doctor and sheer genetic luck, but may in fact depend just as much on how healthy you decide to be. Research suggests that a positive outlook, moderation and willingness to adapt are highly significant factors in a person's ability to maximize their healthy lifespan.

B Towards a definition of 'successful ageing'

Weigand, M. (2008). *Journal of Well-being, 2*, 238–239.

Life expectancy at birth has been increasing steadily since the early twentieth century. This has implications for governments and health policy specialists who must plan for increased medical costs and social care. Perhaps unsurprisingly, there has been renewed interest in the idea of encouraging people to 'age successfully' – that is, to maintain healthy behaviours throughout life, particularly in middle adulthood, to experience as much of one's lifetime as possible free from serious disease or disability. There is some debate about whether increases in longevity mean an overall improvement of human life, or mean that morbidity, serious illness and disability are merely 'put off' until later (Mor, 2005). However, several recent studies indicate that improvements in medical care and a shift in the types of illness which afflict the elderly mean that more people now enjoy a greater portion of their life free from serious disability.

This improvement could be enhanced still further by a proactive policy of encouraging healthy behaviours throughout one's life in order to maximize the proportion of it that is spent in good health. This brief study attempts a definition of 'successful' ageing based on a review of recent literature on the topic.

Three models of successful ageing

The literature presents three main strands of thought about what it means to age successfully. Some studies have defined it mainly as a medical issue, focusing on the absence of disease throughout the lifespan of the individual. A second model of successful ageing emerges from studies which focus on psychological and societal factors such as a personal sense of well-being and satisfaction. A third view of what constitutes successful ageing comes from investigating the opinions of the elderly themselves, who are found to have their own definitions of what it means to have aged well, although often these represent an overlap of the two purely theoretical models described above.

The medical view portrays successful ageing as the absence of long-term or significant disability or disease, or the factors which contribute to it. These include general good health, avoidance of high-risk behaviours such as drinking or smoking, staying mentally and physically active, and maintaining autonomy (Rowe and Kahn, 1998). This has been the most commonly accepted definition of the term 'successful ageing', at least by government and medical community standards, not least because it neatly defines 'correct' behaviours and is statistically measurable. However, it has been claimed that the Rowe and Kahn model is somewhat unrealistic because it does not take into account the fact that the majority of people will be unable to enjoy an old age free of disease. Elderly people who consider themselves to have aged well based on their own criteria may not be considered to have done so under the strict medical definition of the term. This begs the question of whose definition should be accepted.

Psychosocial models go some way towards broadening the medical model definition, including as they do measures of individual life satisfaction. Thus an elderly person who suffers from a chronic disability may still consider themselves to have aged well if they are able to cope despite the disability. It is a fact that the vast number of people will still suffer from some disease or disability as they age, and so the psychosocial model allows a definition of successful ageing which includes illness, if the individual is able to enjoy a standard of autonomy and satisfaction despite suffering it.

As a common definition of successful ageing, then, despite disease or disability, it is still possible to investigate an individual's 'health' in terms of their satisfaction with life. This includes their happiness, determination to enjoy life, morale, sense of self-worth, overall mood, enjoyment of fulfilling relationships and optimism about the future. The psychosocial model can also be extended to include the ability to participate in society, and the sense of worth which this brings. The psychosocial model, and the associated concept of 'wellness', is also proving a popular model of success among policymakers, as it allows them to formulate programmes to encourage individuals to take an optimistic, self-reliant approach to their own health.

Bowling and Dieppe (2005) cite a number of studies which have investigated older people's own opinions of what it means to age successfully. These definitions tend to show an overlap with the two models described above, though the emphases tend to vary widely between individuals. These include expected factors like autonomy, physical health, satisfaction with life, financial and physical security, spirituality, emotional comfort and the presence of loved ones, as well as more unexpected and individual assertions such as a sense of humour, consumption of particular foodstuffs or beverages, or specific pastimes. Bowling and Dieppe's study indicated that 75% of older respondents thought of themselves as ageing 'very well' or 'well', though in the strict medical model a large percentage of these respondents would be classed as not ageing successfully. Nevertheless, they report that the most common definition of successful ageing cited by elderly respondents was physical health.

Conclusion

A broad definition of successful ageing which includes both psychosocial as well as lay opinions of contributing factors alongside simple absence of disease has several implications for healthcare policymakers. The three models of ageing described above are not mutually exclusive by any means, but their use in isolation tends to reflect the disciplinary background of the people who are using them. Providers of healthcare have tended to focus too narrowly on the purely medical definition of successful ageing. In fact, medical staff need to understand patients' views of what it means to age well, and be sensitive to the fact that they may have needs which go beyond the merely physical in order to consider themselves well.

As both the psychosocial and lay views identify social functioning – playing a role in society – as an important aspect of successful ageing, it would seem appropriate to encourage people to establish strong social networks from an early age, and to assist them in maintaining access to these networks as they grow older. Related to this is the necessity of providing a range of community services which can support social activities.

Recent years have seen a rise in the idea of wellness – a measure of health which considers how emotionally and physically satisfied a person is, rather than merely on the absence of sickness. Though healthcare provision based on this field of study has yet to win widespread popular acceptance, it may ultimately bring considerable benefits if it becomes part of the accepted notion of what it means to live a healthy life.

References

Bowling, A. and Dieppe, P. (2005). What is successful ageing and who should define it? *British Medical Journal, 331*, 1548–51.

Mor, V. (2005). The compression of morbidity hypothesis: a review of research and prospects for the future. *Journal of the American Geriatric Society, 53*, S308–9.

Rowe, J.W. and Kahn, R.L. (1998). *Successful Aging*. New York: Pantheon Books.

Go to the checklist on p.179. Look again at the tips relating to Unit 4 Part A and tick (✓) those you have used in your studies. Read the tips relating to Unit 4 Part B.

By the end of Part C you will be able to:
- keep detailed records
- record correct bibliographic information
- keep a detailed scientific logbook
- establish the relevance of abstracts
- identify common features of abstracts
- use an abstract for research.

1 Keeping detailed records

In the course of your studies you will probably have to keep a record of information. For science students, this could mean keeping a logbook of laboratory work, while for others it might mean taking notes to help write an essay or report.

1a Decide whether each statement about keeping records is true (T) or false (F) for you.

1 I take notes on note-cards, which I keep together.

2 I prefer to take notes in a notebook – I tend to lose individual sheets of paper.

3 I usually don't take notes – I prefer to highlight my own copy of a text directly.

4 I don't have a special technique for taking notes – I just write down information in any way I like.

5 I use different coloured pens to show different types of information, such as quotes and paraphrases.

6 I always keep a record of bibliographic information for any sources I am using.

7 I occasionally lose important records.

8 I have a system for organizing my records.

9 I use a laptop or tablet computer to take notes.

1b Compare your answers with a partner and discuss any differences. What are the advantages and disadvantages of some of the techniques described in 1a?

When you are doing research, whether in a lab or using written texts, it is important to keep your records accurate. This might include the following:

- Making a note of bibliographic data – where did the information come from? You will need to write a reference for any information you use, so it's good to keep a record now.

- Making sure that you write the page numbers that the information comes from, because you may need this to write a citation in an essay or report.

- Clearly showing what the notes are – for example, make sure that notes written in your own words are distinct from quotations.

- Keeping your notes in one place, such as a notebook, or bound together, so that you can find information again quickly.

1c These notes were written by a student researching the subject of malaria for an essay. Read the notes and write down problems the student might have when he/she uses the notes for an essay.

Source – World Health Org. report
There were an estimated 247 million malaria cases among 3.3 billion people at risk in 2006.
- Many tools and methods to stop malaria including:
  - nets
  - insecticide
  - treatment (medicine)
Most malaria victims are children.
Many countries → Africa → malaria rates ↓

Problems with the notes

1d Read the notes made by another student on the same topic. Identify the things they have done well. Write notes about any things you will try to do in your own note-taking.

Source : World Health Organisation
World Malaria Report
2008 / Geneva / WHO Press
Available on → WHO website → http://apps.who.int/Malaria/

109 countries where malaria is endemic (p. 9)
Africa – 647 mil. people at risk
S.E. Asia – 1319 mil.   "   "   "   } (p. 10)
Euro. – 22 mil.   "   "   "

My comment :
Serious divide between developing + developed.

"There were an estimated 247 million malaria cases worldwide in 2006." (p. 10)

Good ideas from the notes

2 Recording correct bibliographic information

> In Unit 1 Part C you looked at the Harvard referencing system. At the end of any report or essay, it is usually necessary to write a list of references to acknowledge any sources that you have used or referred to. Making an accurate reference list is a painstaking job, and it can take a very long time. It is a good idea to write down all the bibliographic information that you will need for the reference list as soon as you start taking notes from a source.

2a Before continuing with this section, review the information about Harvard style references in Unit 1 Part C, section 3.

2b Look at these three examples of notes. Look carefully at the types of source and the bibliographic details for each one. What information has each student forgotten to include?

1

Author – Charles Poser + George Bruyn
Book – An illustrated history of malaria
Date – 1999

Name 'Malaria' from Italian

'Mal' 'aria' = 'Bad Air' (p. 21)
↓
Comes from idea that malaria is associated with unhealthy air in swamps. (p. 21 - 23)

2

AUTHOR : STEVE CONNOR
TITLE : BREAKTHROUGH IN FIGHT AGAINST MALARIA
NEWSPAPER : THE INDEPENDENT
TUESDAY 7TH APRIL 2009

MALARIA → ONLY FROM FEMALE MOSQUITOS

MOSQUITOS → NEED WATER TO LAY EGGS
↓
CARRY MALARIA PARASITE
CALLED PLASMODIUM

Authors : Ria Malaney, Andrew Spielman, Jeffrey Sacks

Journal article : The Malaria Gap

Journal title : American Journal of Tropical Medicine + Hygiene

---

General thesis – serious gap in treatment for rich and poor people (my interpretation)

p. 143 – Malaria "inhibits long term growth"
→ It causes economic problems in poor countries.
→ Countries too poor to treat it get extra burden.

3 Keeping a detailed scientific logbook

If you are studying a subject that requires you to work in a laboratory, then an important type of written record is a logbook. This is something like a diary that you write while you are in the lab, recording what you have done and the results you observed as well as your comments or questions. This logbook is then used to write a formal lab report after you have finished your work. The logbook is your record of all the information you will need for your lab report, so it is important that you take very detailed notes about what is happening and write down data clearly and neatly.

The contents of a logbook
A logbook will normally include these sections:

• Introduction and theoretical background

• Methods and materials

• Description of results

• Graphs

• Discussion section

• Conclusion

Before the lab session
You will normally receive a set of instructions (or a lab manual) before you do lab work. This may include instructions for some things that you need to do before the laboratory session begins. You should keep a note of what you do in the logbook. If you don't understand something in the instructions, it is a good idea to write questions in the logbook as well, to ask the teacher during the lab session. It can be useful to prepare blank tables in your logbook before the lab session to make it easy to enter observed data while you are in the lab.

During the lab session

Use your logbook to keep a note of what you do while the experiment proceeds. Normally this will be similar to the lab instructions, but you may do something which is different from the lab instructions. In this case it is very important to make a note of it in your logbook. As the lab session progresses, write down any questions or thoughts that come to mind.

After the lab session

Use your notes to help you write the lab report.

3a Look at these tips about logbook writing and write 'Do' or 'Don't' at the start of each.

1 _____ copy material from your lab manual into the logbook – this is a distraction and a waste of time.

2 _____ spend more than 20–30 minutes per lab session on writing your logbook – the primary aim of the lab session is practical experience.

3 _____ write your results accurately, even if they were not what you expected.

4 _____ record the date and the experiment title at the beginning of each session.

5 _____ write in pen. This gives a permanent record of your results.

6 _____ change or cross out information – even if you make a mistake, it is important to include this in your logbook so that you can learn from it.

7 _____ write anything which happens – even if you think you have made a mistake, it can be a useful record in the future.

8 _____ tear pages out, or stick pages in from elsewhere. Your logbook should be an accurate, permanent record of what happened, so it's important to be honest.

9 _____ write your name, course/group and the name of the laboratory module on the cover of the logbook.

10 _____ always write in full sentences – logbooks in note form are perfectly acceptable.

11 _____ organize the information clearly and tidily – leave plenty of spaces, and use colours, boxes, etc. to differentiate sections.

12 _____ make sure that your language is clear enough for other people to read.

4 Establishing the relevance of abstracts

There are a vast number of academic periodicals, or journals, available to help you research a topic. In fact, there are so many journals that simply finding the information you are looking for can be difficult. This is where abstracts and abstract databases can help.

The function of abstracts
Students in all academic fields and at all levels are expected to do a lot of reading. When your teacher gives you a reading list, this is not such a problem. However, when you are doing secondary research on a subject you will have to find relevant sources by yourself. The problem then becomes having enough time to find sources and deciding if they are suitable or not, even before you have read them thoroughly.

Most journal articles include an abstract. This is a short summary which usually appears at the front of the article. It shows the key information contained in the article and can help you decide quickly if the article is suitable for your purpose or not.

Abstract databases
Most university libraries and websites now have access to online databases, which make it easy to scan through many journal archives for a particular keyword. Usually the database will let you view the abstracts of the articles that it finds, which you can read quickly to decide if the article it has found is what you need.

There are general abstract databases as well as subject-specific ones. The general databases, such as *Web of Knowledge*, can search through a huge number of journal articles on all sorts of topics, while the subject-specific ones are useful if you are looking for a specific type of journal article. No database is perfect, so it is good to become familiar with both types, and use a mixture of them when you search for sources.

4a Work in pairs. Look at the extract from a list of abstract databases on p.154. Discuss these questions.

1 Which database(s) would you use to help you search for sources for an essay about culture and language?

2 Which database(s) would you use to help you search for sources for a chemistry project?

3 Which databases would be of most use to life-sciences students?

4 Which database could be used to search for information on any topic?

5 Which database could you use if you were searching for information about the historical development of British English?

Database title	Description
Aerospace & high technology database	Aeronautics and space science
Anthropological index online	Database from the Museum of Mankind
British history online	General history of the British Isles
Chemical database service	Chemistry-related topics
CSA Illumina	Cambridge Sciences Collection
JSTOR Biological Sciences collection	Biology-related topics
Linguistics & language behaviour abstracts	Language study topics
MathSciNet	Mathematics
MEDLINE	Medical sources
SciFinder Scholar	Chemistry abstracts
Sociological abstracts	Sociology and behavioural science
Structural genomics knowledgebase	Research data on genomics and structural biology
Web of Knowledge (WoK)	Database for various sources

5 Identifying common features of abstracts

> Abstracts, like any academic writing, can be written in many different ways. However, many abstracts tend to include either some or all of this information:
>
> a A brief introduction to the topic
> b A statement of a problem
> c A description of the methodology used to do the research
> d A summary of results or findings
> e A conclusion about what has been found or what the findings suggest
> f A statement of the author's aim in writing the paper.

5a Look at these sample abstracts. Identify which of the above features (a–f) you find in each abstract.

1

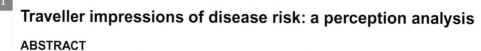

Traveller impressions of disease risk: a perception analysis

ABSTRACT

With a worldwide increase in travel, the speed with which highly infectious diseases can spread around the world has become an extremely important topic. However, the literature on travel and health lacks analysis of prevailing impressions of risk held by tourists. Therefore, this research, recently carried out in the USA, attempts to outline tourists' impressions of the risk they face individually from infectious diseases while travelling abroad, on the one hand, and the impact of high-speed air travel on disease spread on the other. Positive and negative attitudes to health and travel are presented, and an overview of perceived risk factors influencing travel decisions is given.

Although the results strongly suggest that most travellers underestimate the danger of diseases spreading through air transport, there is a high degree of awareness of individual risk. With the findings it is hoped to provide a better insight into the impressions held by potential tourists of health dangers from infectious disease and to help those engaged in providing healthcare to identify an efficient strategy for containing and treating the spread of disease.

Hiller, A. (2007). Traveller impressions of disease risk: a perception analysis. *Tropical Health Journal, 63*, 159–172.

2

Patient preference and the availability of healthcare services in rural Somerset

ABSTRACT

The tendency to view patients as consumers has become fashionable within healthcare throughout the developed world. This is also the case in the UK, where medical care is offered as a menu of 'choices' to NHS patients. Doctors' clinics compete for patients, and patients can choose another doctor if they are not satisfied. The aim of this is to give medical professionals an incentive to offer high-quality services. In order for such a system to operate successfully, there must be a large enough range of medical services on offer to make the 'choice' truly meaningful. This study investigated the quantity and availability of medical choices in a rural area of south-west England. Data was gathered from two NHS surveys of the Somerset region in the years 2001 and 2006. It was found that the range of doctors' surgeries available was limited in both number and geographical location. Patients do try to take advantage of choice if it is available, though this depends on mobility. Their reasons for choosing to change to a different doctor's surgery include poor standard of care, perception of better services at a different location, and difficulty in booking appointments at convenient times. The findings suggest that treating patients as 'consumers' by offering them choice in this way can improve patient access to general health services, as well as provide incentives for doctors to provide a good service, but this depends on having enough medical practices available in a given area. Rural residents in the UK suffer from a lack of real choice compared to city dwellers.

Gorman, P. & Martins, A.K. (2007). Patient preference and the availability of healthcare services in rural Somerset. *Healthcare Policy Professional, 3*, 22–26.

3

The coming century: global healthcare challenges and opportunities

ABSTRACT

The twentieth century has seen great advances in primary healthcare provision worldwide, with success in improving nutrition, combating preventable diseases and reductions in mortality. However, the twenty-first century will see emerging challenges for public healthcare. The current paper identifies three major areas which the World Health Organisation has identified as presenting challenges to the medical community in the coming century. Most of these challenges are connected to background socio-economic status and are exacerbated by overpopulation and climate change.

Undoubtedly, the three main medical challenges which the world will face in the coming years are: good nutrition, including both provision of sufficiently nourishing food in the developing world, as well as limiting the effects of over-consumption in the richer nations; the provision of medical services to regions of conflict; the containment of highly infectious or dangerous diseases such as AIDS. We emphasise the seriousness of these challenges and the need for timely action to avoid regional health crises.

Key Words: Health; Medical challenges; Nutrition; Conflict; Disease control

Croft, B. A., & Gallagher, R. (2002). The coming century: global healthcare challenges and opportunities. *Canadian Medical Digest*, *107*, S301–S339.

5b Check your answers with a partner.

6 Using an abstract for research

6a You have to write an essay with the title *Examine the impact of climate change on human health.* Work in pairs. Discuss the title. Then make a short plan for your essay.

> **Essay plan: Examine the impact of climate change on human health**

6b Read these abstracts and decide which ones could help you with the essay and why / why not.

1

Analyzing the effects of climate change on agricultural land in Sub-Saharan Africa

ABSTRACT

The Intergovernmental Panel on Climate Change predicts that average global temperatures will increase by 5°C or beyond. If this happens as the IPCC has projected, suitable farmland for growing maize will decrease in Sub-Saharan Africa, where it forms a staple crop in many regions. This will be compounded by an increase in the incidence of severe drought events. As the temperature increases, regions which have moderate-fertility soils will suffer greatly. In addition to the reduction of suitable agricultural land for maize growth overall, the IPCC predictions suggest that this change will be felt most severely in areas which are already under economic strain. The current IPCC predictions suggest that this scenario is likely, but that mitigation is possible with sufficient funding.

Al-Ibrahim, S., & Rocha, W. (2002). Analyzing the effects of climate change on agricultural land in Sub-Saharan Africa. *Climate Modelling*, *22*(2), 141–162.

2 Does climate change have negative impacts on the health of arthropod populations?

ABSTRACT

The situation of arthropods in a rapidly changing climate is currently unclear. The versatility and abundance of arthropod life-forms suggests that they are able to adapt successfully to even hostile environments. However, recent studies suggest that some arthropod species may in fact be endangered if climate change projections are correct. The present paper compares the latest information from a number of studies conducted within the last two years and considers the implications for species conservation. Arthropod populations which are more resilient due either to greater numbers or adaptability may be resistant to climate change impacts. However, there is a consensus that certain species are more vulnerable, either due to direct effects on health, or the destruction of their natural habitats or food sources. Attempts by conservationists to respond to the climate change risk should begin with a thorough assessment of the level of threat to arthropod population health. More research is needed.

Feltham, G. & Hudson, W. (2008).
Does climate change have negative impacts on the health of arthropod populations?
Biological Enquiry, 87, 1604–1619.

3 Assessing the extent of the climate change risk to human welfare

ABSTRACT

The present study reviews the scientific basis of claims about climate change and examines future climate change projections from the IPCC. Potential impacts on the physical and social environment, as well as health and welfare, are explored, leading to an assessment of the extent to which climate change can be said to present a serious threat to continued human welfare. The article considers the merits of different proposals for avoidance or mitigation of climate change, comparing speculative 'high-tech' solutions with a shift to a low-carbon economy. The study concludes with a presentation of the likely welfare consequences of failure to mitigate climate change.

McCauley, N. (2009). Assessing the extent of the climate change risk to human welfare. *Social Factors*, 14, 207–214.

4 Evidence for climate change impacts on health

ABSTRACT

The effects of climate change will have a significant impact on human health. The years ahead are likely to see an increase in impacts ranging from the relatively innocuous, such as heat-related discomfort, eventually to severe injury and death. A major contributor to poor health in a warming world will be the production and spread of serious or even fatal infectious diseases. Pollution and extreme weather events will add to the range of health threats in the environment. It is also expected that climate change will reduce the abundance of fresh water for direct consumption, hygiene and agriculture. It will force changes in farming yields and practices, which will increase the problem of nutrition in areas of poor food-security.

Wilson, S. & Goldstein, S. J. (2004). Evidence for climate change impacts on health. *Bulletin of the School of Tropical Medicine*, 62, 543–587.

5

Livestock in a world of climate change: the situation in North America

ABSTRACT

Recent studies have focused on the negative impacts that livestock farming can have on the environment. The production of animal feed requires a great deal of chemical assistance in most cases, which contributes to greenhouse gas (GHG) emissions. The IPCC (Intergovernmental Panel on Climate Change) estimates that 9% of GHGs are generated by livestock through methane and associated effects. A related issue, though one not directly associated with climate change, is the high volume of grain needed to produce a proportionally smaller quantity of meat, which has consequences for nutrition and resource use which will be heightened if climate change affects the quantity of farmland available. Policymakers therefore have a challenging task in attempting to offset the negative effects of raising livestock for food with their food-security and cultural benefits. The current paper analyzes the impact of changes in livestock use in the USA and Canada and considers different impediments to change in the way livestock are raised and consumed in each nation. It examines the approaches that national policymakers are taking in each country to reduce the negative environmental impacts of keeping livestock.

Keywords: livestock; climate change; food; agriculture

Mason, C., Boswell, J. & Potter, A. (2007). Livestock in a world of climate change: the situation in North America. *Fauna*, *4*(3), 607–614.

> **UNIT TASK**   **Health expectancy**

In this unit task, you will continue to research information for one of these titles:

Examine the factors that contribute to increased health expectancy.

or

Compare the health expectancy situation in two countries of your choice.

a Choose one of the titles and decide on the search criteria you will use to find relevant sources.

b Research your chosen essay title. Using a general abstract database such as *Web of Knowledge*, try to find at least two journal articles which are relevant to each topic. (Be aware that *Web of Knowledge* is a general database, so a basic search may return thousands of articles which are not connected to your topic. Spend some time practising how to refine your search so that you only get titles that are likely to be suitable for you.)

Go to the checklist on p.179. Look again at the tips relating to Unit 4 Parts A–B and tick (✓) those you have used in your studies. Read the tips relating to Unit 4 Part C.

Reporting in speech

By the end of Part D you will be able to:

- define a purpose for a presentation
- be aware of your audience
- give effective pair presentations
- plan and produce a poster.

1 Defining a purpose for a presentation

1a Work in pairs and answer these questions.

1 Why do people give presentations?

2 What was the topic of the last presentation you saw?

3 Look at the diagram below. What was the main purpose of the presentation?

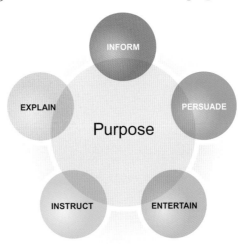

1b Work in pairs. Look at presentations 1–5. Discuss what the purpose of each one might be and say what different features they might have in terms of style, structure, language, etc. Write notes in columns 2 and 3.

Presentation	Purpose	Features
1 A training session on how to use a new computer system	*Instruct*	*Simple language, a step-by-step guide, slow pace, possibly questions throughout, quite formal.*
2 A presentation on culture shock when you arrive at a new university		
3 A presentation as part of a research proposal		
4 A lecture on the evolution of frogs		
5 A speech at a meeting of the Debate Society in the Students' Union		

2 Being aware of your audience

2a You have been given the task of preparing a presentation on the topic of sleep deprivation among students. Work in pairs and discuss the questions in each column of the table below. Then complete columns 2–4.

	Who is your audience?	What does your audience know?	What is your purpose?	How do you adjust your presentation?
1	High school students	They know about the importance of sleep but maybe not know about the effects of sleep deprivation	The purpose is to inform (and perhaps persuade)	Make the language simpler to understand. Include examples relevant to teenagers. More anecdotal and personalized
2	A lecture to a group of nurses			
3	A presentation in class for an assignment			
4	A group of parents of teenagers			
5	A presentation to a politician to change the law			

4.8

2b Listen to a presentation and answer these questions.

1 Is the presentation formal or informal? Can you give examples to support your answer?

2 Do you think the audience is
- a group of high school students?
- a group of nurses?
- fellow students?
- a group of teenagers' parents?
- a politician?

3 How does this affect the style and content? Try to notice examples as you listen.

3 Giving effective pair presentations

3a Write notes on your ideas in the table on p.161.

1 How are group/pair presentations different from individual presentations?

2 What advantages do they have?

3 What disadvantages are there?

Notes on group/pair presentations	
Advantages	Disadvantages

Before giving a pair presentation, you need to plan your tasks. In order to save time and avoid doing the same things twice, it is important to share the work between you. You also need to plan the delivery of your presentation carefully. You need to consider seating arrangements, handovers (when you stop talking and invite your partner to start), overall presentation structure, introductions and conclusions. You also need to think about what visuals you will use and how this can be organized. This is especially important if you are being assessed. It is easy for the audience to see if different parts of a presentation do not fit together.

3b Look at the tasks in this table. Which tasks are best done in pairs, and which can be done individually? Tick (✓) the correct column.

	Pair work	Individual
1 Choosing your topic		
2 Gathering the information		
3 Deciding the focus		
4 Planning the structure		
5 Deciding what to include for each individual part		
6 Preparing the visual aids		
7 Practising the presentation		

3c Work in pairs. Number the stages for delivering a pair presentation in the correct order.

a One speaker explains how the talk will be divided and who will talk about each part. He/She confirms that there will be time for questions afterwards and then hands over to the second speaker.

b One speaker introduces himself/herself and the other speaker.

c One speaker sums up the talk and perhaps makes a conclusion. The audience is invited to ask questions.

d The first speaker introduces and talks about the first section. He/She then hands over to the second speaker.

e The second speaker introduces and talks about the second section.

f One speaker introduces the topic of the talk.

4.8

3d Listen again to the pair presentation and answer these questions.

1 Does each person take an equal role or is there one person who does more or less than the other?

2 What language do they use to hand over?

3 How does each part link with the next one?

3e Look at the advice for giving pair presentations. Tick any things that you already do. Circle two things that you would like to try doing next time you give a presentation.

1 Set roles so you are clear on what you are expected to do.

2 Practise the presentation together.

3 Share the preparation equally.

4 Choose your topic together.

5 Have regular meetings to make sure that your preparation is on track.

6 Allow for clear and fluid handovers.

7 Make sure the presentation is divided equally so both speakers do and say about the same amount.

8 Watch examples of pair presentations online and get ideas about how to improve.

9 If you are using visual aids such as PowerPoint, work to produce the slides together so that they look consistent.

10 Practise timing yourselves as you deliver the presentation.

3f Compare your answers with a partner. Think of some more advice.

4 Planning and producing a poster

> In science and engineering subjects, it is highly likely that you will be asked to do a poster presentation.

4a Look at this definition of a poster presentation from a student handbook. How are poster presentations different from other types of presentation?

> A scientific poster is a visual display of technical information. The presenter is not necessarily required to make a formal presentation, but to answer questions and provide further details about the information in the poster.

> There is limited space in a poster presentation so an important skill is deciding what content you need to include and which should be omitted.

4b Work in groups and look at the sample posters on p.163 and p.164. Half of you should look at poster A on p.163, half of you poster B on p.164. Complete the relevant column on p.165 with notes on the poster's features.

4c Work in pairs with somebody who looked at a different poster from you. Tell your partner about the features of your poster.

Poster A

DISCUSS THE CONTRIBUTION THAT FOSSIL FUELS HAVE MADE TO MODERN HUMAN SOCIETY AND CONSIDER THEIR ENVIRONMENTAL IMPLICATIONS

Introduction

There are many implications that fossil fuels have made to modern human society and the environment.

This paper assesses fossil fuels' contributions to human society, and risks of fossil fuels in the environment.

Detail introduction of oil and coal

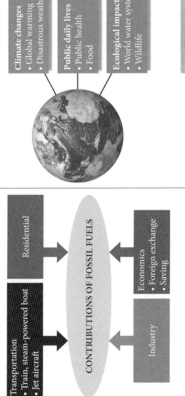

- Hydroelectric
- Natural gas
- Coal
- Petroleum
- Non-hydro renewable
- Nuclear power

Figure 1: Six primary sources of fossil fuel consumptions

Chow, J., Kopp, R.J. and **Portney, P.R.** (2003), *Energy Resources and Global Development* VOL 302 SCIENCE

This bar chart is used to show benefits of fossil fuels. According to the bar chart, there are six primary sources of global energy consumptions.

Fossil fuels' contribution to human society

Transportation
- Train, steam-powered boat
- Jet aircraft

Industry

Residential

Economics
- Foreign exchange
- Saving

CONTRIBUTIONS OF FOSSIL FUELS

The contributions that fossil fuels have made to modern human society are a. o. industry, transportation, residential and economics.

Industry

The Chemical Industry
- Basic chemicals
- Chemical products used in further manufacture
- Finished chemical products

The Steel Industry
- Use coal and natural gas for energy

Fossil fuels are primary sources for industry. The two main usages of fossil fuels in industry are the chemical industry and the steel industry.

Environmental Impacts

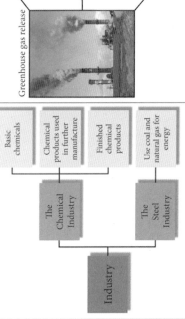

Climate changes
- Global warming
- Disastrous weather

Public daily lives
- Public health
- Food

Ecological impact
- World water systems
- Wildlife

Greenhouse gas release

Influence wildlife

Do harm to human beings

Climate changes and world water system

Conclusion

To sum up: Fossil fuels play a very important role in the modern society. Fossil fuels not only occupy an important position to promote the industrial and transportation development, scientific and technological progress, they are also used widely in people's daily lives.

However, the use of fossil fuels has brought disadvantages to the environment such as global climate change, harm to public health and wildlife.

Reference

Chow, J, Kapp, R.J and Portney, PR. (2003), *Energy Resources and Global Development* VOL 302 SCIENCE

David, J., Tenenbaum (2006), *Food vs. Fuel. Diversion of Crops Could Cause More Hunger*, VOL 116 No. 6, Environmental Health Perspectives

Industrial Energy Use (Washington D.C., U.S. Congress, Office of Technology Assessment, OTA E. 196, June 1983)

J. Environ. Monit. (2005), *Environmental health implications of global climate change*, The Royal Society of Chemistry

Kennesaw State University, *ESA21 Environmental Science Activities for the 21st Century, Fossil Fuels, Coal*, Retrieved January 21st 2009 from World Wide Web: http://esa21.kennesaw.edu/activities/coal/coalactivity.pdf

Sarvesh, Kumar Tiwari (2007), *Oil Spill Disasters and Sethusamudram*, Retrieved March 21st 2009 from World Wide Web http://www.scribd.com/doc/2230613/Oil-Spill-and-Sethusamudram

U.S. Congress, Office of Technology Assessment, *Fuelling Development, Energy Technologies for Developing Countries*, OTA-E-516 (Washington D.C., U.S. Government Printing Office. April, 1982)

U.S. Congress, Office of Technology Assessment, *The Direct Use of Coal* (Washington D.C., U.S. Government Printing Office, April, 1979)

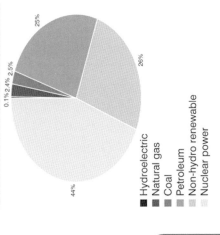

PRODUCT FAILURE

INTRODUCTION

• **In the UK**

In 2002 more than 3000 people died at or around home. Every year about 3 million turn up at emergency departments seeking treatment.

THE CAUSE OF FAILURE

■ Poor product design 43%
■ Unreasonable choice of material 1%
■ Management problems 10%
■ Theoretical mistakes 36%
■ Extreme conditions 7%
■ Others 3%

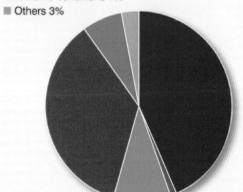

The cause of failure (May & Decker, 2008)

HUMAN ERRORS

• **Poor product design** (club hammer)

A tool that has been widely used in people's everyday life. The sharp edges of the striking face are really dangerous.

(Gregg, 2005)

• **Unreasonable choice of material** (facade failure)

The classic case of a faulty facade is inadequate brick. Both reliability and durability are largely dependent on the quality of materials.

• **Management problems** (management and communication)

Ensure that employees are enabled to use the right mix of skills. Good communication between all levels of employees.

EXTERNAL FACTORS

• **Theoretical mistakes** (perpetual motion machine)

It is impossible to build a perpetual motion device. This design is against the laws of thermodynamics.

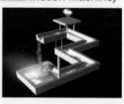

(Ord-Hume, 2006)

• **Extreme conditions** (wind tunnel tests)

High wind created negative pressures on the 60-storey Chase Manhattan Bank Building. Some 15 panes were shattered and caused serious injury to passers-by.

• **Others** (consumer needs)

The picture phone which was introduced in 1964 was a failed design because of lack of demand. Designers fail to understand consumer needs. Product managers use market surveys to help identify consumer attitudes and preferences.

CONCLUSION

A good designer should consider things from every angle especially some details. Combinations of these causes can also contribute to failure in engineering design.

References

• Ross, S. (1984) Material and Methods. *Construction Disasters*. New York: McGraw Hill.

• Gagg, C. (2005) Domestic Product Failures – case studies. *Engineering Failure Analysis, 12,* 784/807.

• May, I. L. & Deckker, E. (2008) Reducing the risk of failure by better training and education. *Engineering Failure Analysis*.

• Schultz, R.L. (2001) The role of ego in product failure. University of Iowa.

• Ul-Hamid, A. Tawancy, HM. (2004) *Practical engineering failure analysis*. New York: Marcel Dekker.

• Ord-Hume, AW. J.G. (2006) Perpetual Motion: *The history of an obsession*. Adventures Unlimited Press.

	Poster A	Poster B
Design		
Text		
Pictures and diagrams		
Layout		
Subtitles and headings		

4d Read this advice on making a good poster presentation and complete the second and third columns of the table.

	Agree/Disagree	Why?
1 Keep the material simple.		
2 Use a lot of colours to make your presentation noticeable.		
3 Do not use more than two font types.		
4 Write a clear title.		
5 Use only UPPER CASE letters.		
6 Use headings to organize your presentation.		
7 Use diagrams, pictures and graphs to support your ideas (but not too much).		
8 Make sure to include a lot of text to explain your points.		

4e Work in pairs or in small groups. Plan a poster presentation for the topic *Health expectancy*.

4f Display your poster at the front of the class and answer any questions your classmates have.

4g Evaluate your poster presentation. Does it follow the checklist in 4d?

In this unit task, you will prepare and give a ten-minute pair presentation on health expectancy. For this presentation you will select information for one of the essay titles below that you chose in the unit task in Part C:

Examine the factors that contribute to increased health expectancy.

or

Compare the health expectancy situation in two countries of your choice.

a   Work in pairs. Decide what needs to be done, and plan which tasks each of you will complete.

b   Work in pairs. Discuss the topic of your presentation and formulate a thesis statement. Write your thesis statement below to remind yourself of your goal in the presentation.

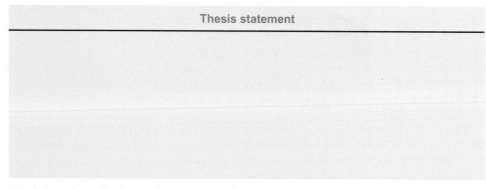

Thesis statement

c   Work in pairs. Divide up the sections of your presentation. The main section should include a summary of the research that you have read, as well as an attempt to persuade your audience about your thesis statement. You can decide together on the best way to present your material. There is no single 'right' way to do it.

d   Plan the tasks that you have been assigned.

e   When both of you have prepared your own sections, practise the whole talk together in order to ensure your timing is accurate and the various stages of the presentation are linked smoothly and effectively.

f   Listen to other pairs give their presentations and make notes of anything you hadn't included in your own presentation. This will be useful when you are working on the final unit task.

Go to the checklist on p.179. Look again at the tips relating to Unit 4 Parts A–C and tick (✓) those you have used in your studies. Read the tips relating to Unit 4 Part D.

Reporting in writing

By the end of Part E you will be able to:

- write an introduction
- write a conclusion
- review your written work.

1 Writing an introduction

1a These statements represent some common perceptions about writing an introduction. Decide which statements you agree with (A) and which you disagree with (D). Be prepared to explain why.

1 We can only start to write the body of an essay when we have finished writing the introduction.

2 It is necessary to repeat the title of the paper in the introduction.

3 It is sometimes possible to start with a rhetorical question, such as *Have you ever thought about how you might improve the way you study?*, for example, when writing the introduction of an academic paper. Such a question can help to attract the interest of the reader.

4 The introduction should be very short.

5 Attracting the interest of the reader is an important function of an introduction.

1b Check your answers with a partner.

As with all forms of writing, an introduction has certain functions or purposes. In general terms, the introduction tries to help the reader understand the rest of the text more easily. The features of introductions may vary. However, most introductions contain some or all of the following:

- Information aimed at focusing the reader's attention (and interest) on the topic of the paper (*purpose statement*)
- A clear indication of the purpose / major aim of the text
- Clarification/definitions of any terms which may be interpreted differently by different readers
- A brief outline of the overall structure of the body of the text
- If relevant, an indication of the writer's stance (*thesis statement*)
- In some cases, a brief summary of any relevant 'background' necessary to understand the text.

1c Study the different features of introductions in the table and then read extracts 1–5 from introductory paragraphs. Match the paragraph number with the features of introductions in the first column.

Feature of introduction	Comments	Example
A direct statement giving the focus of the paper (purpose statement)	A very common feature of an introduction, which clearly indicates to the reader what is to follow. This feature is particularly common in research papers.	3
A general statement about how the topic is going to be approached	This is another very common feature. An aspect or some aspects of the topic are introduced by a statement indicating how they will be analyzed.	5
An outline of the structure of the paper	This is a common feature of an introduction which clearly shows the reader the organization and the various major components of the paper. This helps the reader to follow the paper because s/he knows what to expect before reading the full paper.	1
A definition	This style of opening is often used when the topic of the paper is likely to be unfamiliar to the reader or when one or more terms used in the title could be misinterpreted.	4
A statement of the stance which will be taken in the paper (thesis statement)	This indicates to the reader whether the writer is going to argue from a particular stance or give a balanced examination of all relevant arguments.	2

1 The problems caused by sleep deprivation among young people are really worrying. In this paper, the situation will be introduced, and will be followed by an analysis of the problems. Then, proposed solutions will be given. Finally, these solutions will be evaluated.

2 In this paper, I will argue that it is worth spending resources on health care for the elderly.

3 The purpose of this paper is to examine the advantages and the disadvantages of cloning, and to look at its probable future development.

4 The focus of this paper is virtual healthcare. Virtual healthcare is a system which uses computers and networking software to provide professional health advice in remote or rural areas where doctors cannot often go.

5 To study whether or not yoga classes should be provided (and paid for) by the National Health Service, a multiperspective approach will be adopted. Points of view from different groups, including doctors, patients, the public, professional bodies and government officials, will be examined in detail.

1d Look at the following introduction to an essay entitled *The developments in nuclear technology have increased rather than decreased the potential dangers*. Underline the following:

1   the time period covered: past, present, future or a combination
2   what, where and/or who this research focused on
3   a statement of the stance taken in the paper
4   a more general indication of how the topic is going to be approached

Nowadays, even though nuclear technology is widely used to generate electricity for homes and industry in Western Europe, it is difficult to establish whether or not this is a safe and reliable way to generate electricity. Nevertheless, before reaching the conclusion that nuclear technology is either safe or dangerous, it is necessary to investigate the issue from different perspectives. The focus is placed both upon the effectiveness of the existing safety measures commonly adopted and on the potential dangers to human health.

1e Examine these examples of introductory paragraphs and underline the functions (1–4 in 1d).

The medical condition insomnia, from the Latin 'insomnis' – quite literally meaning sleeplessness – is normally defined as the inability to sleep soundly on three or four nights a week over a period of at least six months. It is estimated that around 8–10% of the population suffer from long-term insomnia, while as much as one-third of the population are believed to be suffering from insomnia at any one time. Current approaches to treatment favour CBT, or cognitive behavioural therapy, as the most effective means of treating chronic insomnia. The present paper attempts to examine the pros and cons of CBT as an insomnia treatment. The paper will start by presenting the background to the issue, followed by an analysis of the suggested justifications for and the arguments against using CBT. The conclusion is then based on this analysis.

Smoking is often seen as unhealthy and can affect not only a smoker's health, but also the health of those around them. However, the negative effects of smoking may be exaggerated. The potential problems can be eliminated. The purpose of this paper is to analyze the implications of banning smoking in public places. This paper argues that valid reasons can be found to justify allowing smoking in public places.

1f You are going to write an introduction for this essay title:

Examine the factors that contribute to increased health expectancy.

Firstly, you should decide which of the functions 1–4 in 1d should be included in your introduction.

Then you should write the introduction.

Then swap your introduction with another student. In the second column, try to identify each function they have used.

Introduction	Notes on functions

2 Writing a conclusion

The conclusion to a paper is one of the most important sections in that it influences the reader's final reaction to the paper as a whole. As much care and thought should be put into writing it as into any other section of the paper.

2a Work in pairs. Discuss and tick (✓) which of these you think would be effective ways to conclude a paper.

1 giving more background information ✗
2 restating the thesis you began with ✓
3 discussing the content of the main body of the paper in greater detail ✗
4 suggesting further areas for research related to your topic ✓
5 briefly summarizing the issues you discussed in the paper ✓
6 summarizing the main points/arguments of the paper ✓
7 giving a further quotation which relates to the one used in the introduction ✗
8 referring back to the definition/statement/details contained in the introduction ✓
9 suggesting a broader application of your thesis ✗
10 suggesting the reader should do something in response to the text (sometimes referred to as a 'call for action') ✓
11 answering the questions that you asked in the introduction ✗
12 making a recommendation based on your research ✓

2b Work in pairs. Study conclusions 1–3 below and answer these questions. Where possible, underline the appropriate sentences.

1 Is there a general summary of the writer's argument?

2 Does the writer give his/her own opinion?

3 If so, how does he/she express this opinion?

4 Can you find a call for action?

5 If so, how does the writer express it?

6 Although you have not read the complete texts, can you infer some of their content from the conclusions?

1

In this paper, I have attempted to examine how the rapid development of the Internet has contributed to poorer health among young people. It is undeniable that the Internet was one of the greatest inventions of the twentieth century; it affects almost all aspects of our daily lives. However, the impact of long periods spent in front of computers must be tackled, otherwise the future burden on healthcare systems will be severe.

2

No matter whether your concern is for your personal health, your children's future, the economic future of the community, or the future of the world's environment, we cannot afford to ignore any attempt to further develop nuclear technology. The discussion has clearly shown that the developments in nuclear technology have increased rather than decreased the potential dangers of such a power source.

3

Nowadays, wherever you go, you can see posters reminding people to get more exercise. Such reminders are also given in the media. It is a fact that people are doing less exercise now than ever before. Unless individuals can be motivated to take exercise more seriously, there will be increasing numbers of people suffering from ill-health.

2c Look back at a conclusion to an essay you have written. Answer questions 1–6 in 2b for your conclusion. If necessary, improve your conclusion.

3 Reviewing your written work

It is important to review your work before you invite others to read it. When you have finished a piece of writing, complete the following checklist. Tick (✓) the *Reviewed* column when you have looked at each aspect, then tick (✓) the *Completed* column when you are happy that it is suitable for others to read. You may wish to copy this checklist and refer to it each time you produce any written work.

	Reviewed	Completed
I have answered the question.		
I have organized my assignment in a logical format.		
I have used an appropriate text structure.		
Each paragraph is well structured.		
Ideas are linked clearly to each other.		
I have used an appropriate tone.		
I have used appropriate technical vocabulary.		
I have used a suitable conclusion.		
My spelling and grammar are correct.		
I have referenced my sources appropriately.		
I have written an accurate bibliography.		

Health expectancy

In this unit task, you will write an essay on one of these two titles you chose in Part C.

Examine the factors that contribute to increased health expectancy.

or

Compare the health expectancy situation in two countries of your choice.

a Make an essay plan using whichever method you prefer.

b Write your essay using the ideas from the texts you have read. Write approximately 750 words. Wherever possible, use paraphrasing, summarizing and quotations to support your answer. You should give citations for your sources, e.g. (Downey, 2007), and try to format a list of references at the end using the Havard style.

Go to the checklist on p.179. Look again at the tips relating to Unit 4 Parts A–D and tick (✓) those you have used in your studies. Read the tips relating to Unit 4 Part E.

Review

a Now that you have completed *Skills for Study Level 1*, turn back to the questionnaire on p.6. Consider your responses to the questions now and write your current answers in the fourth column. Think about what you have learned during your study of the book, particularly about approaches to learning, as well as your experiences while completing the assignments and activities.

b Work in pairs. Discuss your answers to the questions below and explain any changes that you have made. Make a plan for how to keep improving your study skills in future.

> **What new skills have you learned that you want to continue using in future?**

What can you do to improve your study habits in each of the following areas?

Listening

Speaking

Reading

Writing

Learning independently

The purpose of this academic skills course is to help you study successfully. To what extent have you transferred the skills you learned here to your other courses? How?

Good study practice checklists

Unit 1 – Approaches to learning

Part A Listening		Tick (✓) if you have followed suggestion
	1 Ask lecturers' permission to record their lectures, then listen again at home.	☐
	2 Pre-read on the topic of your next class and make notes of possible key vocabulary.	☐
	3 Take notes, then improve your understanding by reviewing and organizing them.	☐
	4 Ask questions to confirm your understanding or to get help.	☐
	5 Check with a classmate that you understand instructions.	☐
	6 Practise listening to online lectures and taking notes.	☐
Part B Reading	1 Think about which texts are most suitable for your purpose.	☐
	2 Identify and highlight key points as you read.	☐
	3 Analyze key points and ensure you fully understand them.	☐
	4 Make sure your notes on the text(s) are clear and well organized. Give details of their sources.	☐
Part C Investigating	1 Try to follow the 'effective learning' strategies you discussed in section 1.	☐
	2 Identify the different types of sources on your course reading lists.	☐
	3 Practise using the library catalogue to search for sources.	☐
	4 Find the titles of some journals which might be useful in your course.	☐
	5 In your library, look for research skills guides.	☐

Part D Speaking	1	Read up on subjects before a discussion. Take notes and make a list of questions to discuss.	☐
	2	Use a suitable technique to generate and organize your ideas before a tutorial.	☐
	3	Participate actively in tutorials.	☐
	4	Make notes of what was discussed during the task.	☐
	5	Ask questions to confirm your understanding or to get help.	☐

Part E Writing	1	Analyze assignment titles or questions carefully.	☐
	2	Develop a clear thesis statement to help give your essay purpose.	☐
	3	Organize your ideas clearly by making a plan.	☐
	4	Use information from expert sources to support your ideas.	☐
	5	Give citations for any information you use in the main body of the text.	☐
	6	Write a full reference list for sources of information at the end of your essay.	☐
	7	Check that your finished essay covers all the main points and has a logical structure.	☐
	8	Proof-read your writing for grammatical and spelling mistakes.	☐
	9	Ask a friend to read the first draft of your assignment and make suggestions.	☐

Unit 2 – Communication

Part A Listening		
	1	Before lectures, take time to predict what you will hear. ☐
	2	Organize your notes in a way that helps you understand the information easily. ☐
	3	To what extent do you agree or disagree with what the lecturer is saying? Why? ☐
	4	Make notes of questions that you want to ask, and ask them! ☐
	5	Note the names of any writers or researchers that the lecturer mentions and research them independently. ☐
	6	Use abbreviations and symbols to save time when note-taking. ☐

Part B Reading		
	1	Think about who the writer is. What is their intended purpose? Who is their intended audience? ☐
	2	As you read, consider whether a text is suitable for your purpose. ☐
	3	Analyze key points. Do you agree or disagree with the writer's opinion? Why? ☐

Part C Investigating		
	1	If a problem comes up, encourage group members to deal with it together. ☐
	2	Look in your library for books about group work skills. ☐
	3	Search online for ideas about how to make your group work more effective. ☐
	4	After doing a group task, take some time by yourself to analyze how successful it was and review your role and contribution. ☐

Part D Speaking		
	1	Keep your presentation simple. ☐
	2	Practise with a friend beforehand. ☐
	3	Give a clear and interesting introduction. ☐
	4	Use signposting phrases to indicate the key information in your presentation. ☐
	5	Invite questions from the audience and respond clearly. ☐

Part E Writing		
	1	When making notes, keep a record of the full reference for each source. ☐
	2	When reading, pay attention to the ways writers handle quotations and summaries. ☐
	3	Keep a record of useful synonyms that might help you with paraphrasing. ☐

Unit 3 – Science and technology in society

Part A Listening		
	1	Make a list of phrases that can help you follow the structure and content of lectures.
	2	Pay particular attention after you hear a new keyword or expression – the speaker may restate/define its meaning in simpler language.
	3	Be an active listener – think about what you are hearing and try to predict what is coming next.
	4	Listen to online speeches or lectures and practise predicting what you will hear.

Part B Reading		
	1	Think about how texts are organized.
	2	Use a number of different sources.
	3	Make notes of any good ideas you find.
	4	Ensure you have ways of dealing with the challenges of academic reading.
	5	Think about your reason for reading a text before starting to read.

Part C Investigating		
	1	Ensure your sources are appropriate for your purpose.
	2	Use headings and subheadings to help you choose which parts of a text to focus on.
	3	Check contents pages and indexes to help you find useful information in a text.
	4	Before using an index or contents page, brainstorm the key words that you want to search for.

Part D Speaking		
	1	Think about your audience and what they expect from your presentation.
	2	Organize your presentation into a logical and clear progression of ideas.
	3	Think about different ways to present information. Use a variety of visual aids.
	4	Ensure all your visual aids serve a genuine purpose.

Part E Writing		
	1	Make a clear statement in your introduction.
	2	Write a topic sentence for each paragraph.
	3	Develop your ideas clearly and logically.

Unit 4 – Health issues

Part A
Listening

1   Listen for signposting phrases which show sequence and topics. Keep a list of useful phrases.

2   When you hear signposting phrases, use them to help you analyze the speaker's purpose.

3   Question what the speaker's attitude to the information is, whether you agree or disagree, and why.

Part B
Reading

1   Read a range of sources and compare information.

2   Summarize key points to help develop your understanding.

3   Avoid plagiarism while summarizing – begin by taking notes in your own words.

Part C
Investigating

1   Keep detailed records of your work (e.g. in a scientific logbook or notes).

2   When you take notes from any source, write down a correct bibliographical reference.

3   If you photocopy something from a book or journal, make sure that you include the page numbers in the copy.

4   As you search for journal articles, use abstracts to help you decide which texts will be useful.

Part D
Speaking

1   Identify a clear purpose for your presentation.

2   When working in pairs, make sure you both have clearly defined roles.

3   Practise handovers in pair presentations.

4   Plan a poster presentation carefully and make sure all the content is relevant.

Part E
Writing

1   Include an outline of your essay in your introduction.

2   Don't include any new points in your conclusion, but sum up your overall argument.

3   Use a checklist to help you review your work thoroughly before you submit it.

Appendices

Appendix 1

Examinations are a well-established feature of most education systems around the world. However, in recent years, their existence has been called into question as a result of the pressure they put students under. In this paper, we will argue that examinations are not, on the whole, beneficial to learning. We will first analyze the effects of examinations on the way students learn. We will then go on to discuss how examinations affect teaching. The final point deals with the psychological problems often caused by examinations.

Examinations have a powerful influence on the approach students take to learning. Biggs (1989) presents evidence to show that the existence of examinations encourages students to take a surface approach to their studies; that is, they memorize enough information to pass examinations but do not enquire more deeply into the subjects they are studying. Some writers claim that examinations provide a target for students to aim for and so help them achieve the highest possible standards (Green et al., 1995). However, if high grades are achieved at the expense of truly effective learning, then they are meaningless. As well as encouraging students to take a superficial learning approach, examinations can also adversely affect approaches to teaching. In some educational systems, the examinations determine what is taught and how it is taught. Fullilove (1992, p.131) makes the point that in many countries:

> Examinations establish the aims and objectives which actually serve as teaching guidelines for schools.

Teachers, then, tend to teach to the requirements of the examinations rather than the needs of their students.

Perhaps the worst consequence of examinations, however, is their harmful psychological influence. While most people would agree that a degree of stress is necessary to achieve one's best performance, examinations can cause severe psychological problems for many students. Proponents of examinations should bear in mind the research findings which suggest that relaxed students tend to perform better in academic tasks than those suffering from anxiety (Corno et al., 1981). Examinations clearly cause stress but, on the other hand, may well not lead to better results.

In this paper, we have attempted to present the argument against examinations by focusing on the negative effects they often have on students. It is undeniable that examinations can have some benefits but, unfortunately, these are outweighed by their very serious drawbacks. The problems caused by examinations are in urgent need of satisfactory solutions if we are to maximize real learning in educational institutions.

REFERENCES

Biggs, J. (1989). Approaches to the enhancement of tertiary teaching. *Higher Education Research and Development, 8*, 7–25.

Corno, L., Mitman, A. & Hedges, L. (1981). The influence of direct instruction on student self-appraisals: A hierarchical analysis of treatment and aptitude-treatment and interaction effects. *American Educational Research Journal, 18*, 39–61.

Fullilove, J. (1992). The tail that wags. *Institute of Language in Education Journal, 19*, 130–141.

Green, C., Smallwood, I., Tong, K., & Wong, K. (1995). *An English Language Enhancement Programme*. Language Centre, Hong Kong University of Science and Technology.

Appendix 2

In terms of the approaches they take to learning, students may be divided into two broad categories: those who adopt a **surface** approach to their studies and those who adopt a **deep** approach (Morgan, 1993). Students who adopt a surface approach are mainly concerned with passing the assessed assignments which follow learning activities and, because of this, they tend to select and memorize information directly relevant to their subject assignments. In sharp contrast to this, students who adopt a deep approach involve themselves much more in the learning. They attempt to relate new information to what they already know. In short, the deep approach is more personal than the surface approach and is less focused on success in examinations and tests. A concrete example should help to make the differences clearer.

A student who likes to take very detailed notes or is anxious to receive a lecturer's handout does this so that he/she can reproduce, accurately and completely, the information transmitted by the lecturer. This technique is very common in the surface approach. For the surface learner, learning is mainly the reproduction of information. The deep learner, however, is more concerned with taking selective notes of main points and will spend time interpreting information rather than memorizing it. The deep learner is also more likely to carry out independent reading on study topics. Surface learners tend to minimize the amount of reading they do. In fact, they usually do enough just to pass the assessment task and no more.

Of course, many students are a mixture of these two extremes. They focus on passing tests and examinations, but also think about their learning and allow it to make changes to their patterns of behaviour. Individual and cultural factors also determine the overall approach to learning.

Individual learning styles

Personality has an important role to play in the development of individual learning style. Researching how individuals go about learning English as a foreign language, Nunan (1991) identified four major types:

Concrete learners. These learners learn best through activity. For this reason, they like games, videos and oral work in groups and pairs.

Analytical learners. These learners like studying grammar and reading. They prefer to study alone.

Communicative learners. These learners like listening to native-speakers, watching English TV programmes and enjoy trying out their English in a variety of situations.

Authority-oriented learners. These learners like the teacher to control all classroom activities. They prefer the study of grammar, vocabulary and writing and are anxious to have rules and meanings explained to them.

Cultural influences on approaches to learning

There has been a great deal of argument about the effects of cultural factors on learning approaches. According to Bond (1991), cultural factors play the most important part in determining learning approach. Bond focuses on Chinese learners and presents evidence to show a predominant learning style shaped largely by cultural factors peculiar to Chinese society. For Bond, Chinese learners tend to be authority-oriented, surface learners. This is due to the traditional Chinese respect for authority and the 'carry-over' effects of the enormous effort of memorization required to master the Chinese script.

Bond's findings, however, conflict with the results of a study by Brookfield (1991), whose subjects were a multicultural group of learners learning English in America. Brookfield found that cultural-ethnic factors were insignificant in determining learning approach compared to individual personality type. Of course, once back in their countries of origin, Brookfield's subjects might well revert to their previous (culturally determined) learning approach. The fact is that culture determines, to a large extent, the way educational institutions function and how the teaching in them is carried out. Unfortunately, this means that individual learning styles (the way in which a learner would learn best) are largely ignored.

REFERENCES
Bond, M. H. (1991). *Beyond the Chinese Face*. Hong Kong: Oxford University Press.
Brookfield, S. D. (1991). *Developing Critical Thinkers*. San Francisco: Jossey-Bass.
Morgan, A. (1993). *Improving your Students' Learning*. London: Kogan Page.
Nunan, D. (1991). *Language Teaching Methodology*. London: Prentice Hall.

Appendix 3: The decline in the number of visitors to London: causes and possible solutions

1   Introduction

This report was requested by Mrs. Gillian Brown, Director of the London Tourist Authority (LTA), on 20 June, 2011. The report is a response to the falling numbers of visitors from overseas to London, a phenomenon which is losing millions of pounds for the UK economy. The main aim of the report is to identify the causes of the decline in tourist numbers and recommend ways to increase these numbers. In the report, we (the members of the Special Taskforce of the LTA) present findings which attempt to explain the decline in the number of visitors from overseas, a decline which can be traced back five years. Following the findings, brief conclusions are drawn and a number of recommendations are made as to how visitor numbers might be increased.

2   Procedure

Data for the report was gathered between July and August, 2011. Primary data was collected by interviewing 2,000 randomly selected overseas visitors to London. Twenty London hotels offering three-star service or above were surveyed in order to determine their room occupancy rates. Secondary data was obtained by extensive reading of relevant newspaper and journal articles.

3 Findings

Perhaps the most important cause of declining numbers of visitors over the past five years has been the lack of Americans willing to take the long flight to the UK. American visitors are clearly concerned about possible terrorist attacks and are increasingly spending their holidays in the US. American visitors tend to occupy top-end hotel accommodation and the drop in their numbers is reflected in the room occupancy rates for superior London hotels. The rates have been in the region of 50–60%.

American fear of terrorism is by no means the only reason behind the declining numbers of visitors. A greater concern is that the expectations of tourists have changed. Tourists demand far more than they used to and are determined to get good value for money. Twenty years ago, seeing a show in London and visiting its many museums and historical places represented excellent value for money. However, prices for visitor-related activities in London are now some of the highest in the world and this fact has impacted more negatively on visitor numbers than perhaps any other single factor.

Another important concern for London is that visitors are becoming increasingly aware of environmental issues and while other cities have been cleaning up their environments, London has lagged behind in environmental initiatives. The air is more polluted than ever from vehicle fumes and the river, although less polluted than previously, is still smelly and littered with countless tonnes of rubbish. The level of noise pollution is also high. Increasingly, tourists are not willing to tolerate a bad environment in the places they visit. As Table 1 below shows, most of the Americans we interviewed stated that, as a direct result of the heavily polluted environment, they would probably not return to London in the future. Nearly three-quarters of the Australians interviewed and more than half the French agreed with these views.

Table 1: negative views on London's physical environment by nationality

Nationality	% of tourists making negative comments on London's environment
American	82
Australian	71
French	59
German	54

The final problem is that London has a reputation abroad for rudeness to visitors. As Table 2 below reveals, service in shops and restaurants and in public services such as transportation is generally considered to be poor compared with other major cities. We asked our interviewees to rate different aspects of service in three cities on a five-point scale (1 = very poor to 5 = excellent).

Table 2: tourists' satisfaction with services in service outlets

Service	London	Singapore	New York
Friendliness and helpfulness of hotel staff	3.3	4.1	4.7
Friendliness and helpfulness of shop assistants	1.2	4.2	3.8
Friendliness and helpfulness of restaurant staff	1.5	3.7	3.9

The overall mean score for London is 2.0, which may be described as 'poor'. Singapore and New York achieved significantly higher overall means. A comparison of tourists' views on the friendliness and helpfulness of shop assistants presents a very unwelcome result for London. Sometimes the service of shop staff is more than just rude; it also involves cheating. People who are cheated are unlikely to return to London and will probably mention their experience to their friends who, in turn, will be put off from visiting London.

4   Conclusion

The findings clearly indicate that tourists are now looking for value for money; they are seeking a complete experience with plenty of attractions to visit, good service, a pleasant environment and all at a reasonable price. Our market research has shown, however, that London's tourist attractions are grossly overpriced and do not offer value for money. It can be concluded that to encourage visitors to stay longer (and hence spend more money) and to get greater numbers to come here, London must develop a new and less polluted tourist-friendly infrastructure with good-value attractions.

5   Recommendations

Since London no longer presents good value for tourists, the London Tourist Authority should increase motivation to visit the city by encouraging London-based businesses that rely on tourism to discount the prices of their goods and services significantly.

American tourists are important to London's economy and to encourage them to return, the LTA should emphasize in its literature that London has suffered no major terrorism events in recent years and that airlines offering flights from America to London have excellent safety records.

Tourists are now far more aware of pollution in all its different forms than was the case ten years ago. London is regarded as having an unacceptable level of air pollution caused by fumes from vehicles. To reduce polluting emissions from cars, the LTA recommends that the government should consider charging motorists heavily for driving in London and should promote the use of public transport in the city.

In view of the poor standard of service experienced by many tourists, we suggest that steps should be taken to improve the attitude of service staff towards tourists. An advertising campaign and rewards for courteous staff would probably help to achieve improvements in this area.

Appendix 4: Working successfully in a group

It is something of a cliché to say that group work brings challenges as well as benefits. Being part of a group which forms itself into a strong team can be a highly satisfying experience; the quality of the work that you produce is often much better than any individual member could have produced alone, and the positive atmosphere in a team which is working well together is itself rewarding. However, most people who participate in group work will have experienced their fair share of things not going well; deadlines missed, stress, arguments and hurt feelings sometimes seem to be the more common experiences of group work. Students who have had a bad experience of working in a group are inclined to have negative feelings about all future group tasks, and either don't participate as fully as they might, or consider it an unwelcome burden. In fact, getting the chance to deal with difficulties successfully is one of the greatest benefits of this type of work, and is perhaps the reason why it is often said that employers value the skills that are developed in group work. These skills – interpersonal and problem-solving skills – are valuable in a wide range of work and study situations, so learning how to develop them is time well spent, even if it sometimes seems that the experience of group work is unpleasant. At its best, a challenging group work situation can help students to develop independence, tolerance, and a pro-active approach to work.

Perhaps the most common difficulty for students in group work relates to problems between group members. One member may be too dominant, declaring themselves the leader and insisting that others follow their instructions; another may avoid work altogether, letting the other students carry them, or letting the group down by failing to contribute work which they were given; for others there might be a clash of personalities, with heated arguments that prevent the group from working properly. As common as these problems are, an equally common response is usually to go to the teacher who set the group work task and complain that something needs to be done about the situation or the person causing problems. This may seem like a sensible strategy for fixing group problems but in fact most teachers are unlikely to offer much help. Part of the challenge of group work is developing the ability to work independently, and this includes the group itself sorting out problems rather than going to the teacher for help. Fixing problems becomes the responsibility of the group.

More successful strategies for sorting intragroup problems include setting and agreeing clear ground rules at the start – how often will you meet? What kinds of behaviour, such as lateness, laziness or rudeness, are unacceptable? – or assigning clear roles to each member. Problems often develop because members are uncertain about what they should be doing, so having a clear role within the group lets each member know how they can contribute. If a particularly difficult situation arises with one or more members of the group, then sitting down together and discussing what is wrong openly, and deciding together how you will fix the problem and move on, is an independent response, and often far more successful than simply going to the teacher and asking them to fix a 'broken' group.

Another important characteristic that group work challenges can help to strengthen is tolerance, the ability to accept differences between people. Being tolerant does not mean that you have to force yourself to agree with other people's ideas or behaviour, but instead means that you can understand that they have different personalities, ideas and ways of doing things. A successful group is tolerant of the differences between its members. Tolerance is necessary when working in any group, particularly in situations where you are discussing ideas or giving feedback about drafts of work. No one likes their work to be criticized, so it is a good idea to give feedback gently. Try to avoid merely pointing out problems with another group member's ideas; instead it is usually better to give suggestions for how ideas can be improved. Remember that your aim is for the success of the group.

Another situation requiring tolerance is when groups of people from different linguistic or cultural backgrounds work together. If your group includes a member whose first language is not the same as the other members, remember that they may need more time to understand discussions, even if they appear to be showing agreement.

A final way in which you can strengthen your own group work skills is to avoid taking a passive approach to the work you are doing. Passivity means allowing things to happen in the group which you strongly feel are wrong, but doing nothing to change them. A passive approach to work means that you are not contributing as much as possible to your group, and the quality of the work you all produce may suffer. The opposite approach is sometimes referred to as a pro-active approach – facing problems openly and working to fix them. Similarly to the situation of multilingual groups described above, if you are the only student in a group who does not speak the same language as the others, and are having difficulty understanding them, it is important to explain to the others if you are having a problem. Keeping quiet because you are shy is a passive response, and may lead to more difficulties, but a pro-active approach will help group members to understand each other more clearly.

A common situation in which group members can be passive is when one member of the group dominates the others, perhaps designating themselves the leader or insisting that things be done their own way. It can be tempting to allow self-appointed leaders to take control of the group if they want, but to do so is to be passive. By allowing one member to make all the key decisions, you may be saving yourself the effort of participating fully, but your group runs the risk that that person's ideas are not as good as they could be, and so your work will suffer as a result.

Passivity can also be a problem when you are faced with the opposite type of group member: the lazy student. If one or more members of your group do not participate, then you may be tempted to just ignore them and take over their portion of the work yourself to be sure that it is done properly. This may seem like the best answer in terms of getting the work done, but it is a passive response because you are allowing them to contribute nothing to your team. The students who are being lazy will learn nothing from this, and are likely to do it again in future. A better response is often to sit down together, as a whole group, to discuss the problem and what needs to be done. A pro-active approach would include planning the task carefully at the beginning, and scheduling regular meetings to review the work you have done.

Group work will always present you with problems, but if your group faces these difficulties together, you help each other to develop a pro-active approach to work, increase tolerance for the differences between members, and can work independently to produce the best work possible.

Appendix 5: South-east Asia (recording script)

As you know, there has been some debate about the causes of the periods of conflict in south-east Asia during the fifteenth and eighteenth centuries. The city of Angkor, for example, in modern Cambodia, declined at this time, and people have thought that it was because of an invasion from Siam, as Thailand was then called. But some recent research, and I do mean recent, has cast doubt on this theory. A team from Columbia University, led by Brendan Buckley, that's B-u-c-k-l-e-y, have looked at weather patterns in the region and they argue that a more likely explanation is a long drought, when monsoon rainfall was well below normal.

Unfortunately, there are no weather records for this period, so the team had to use tree ring data. Are you all clear about that? It's a way of studying the rate of growth of certain trees by looking at the width of the annual rings, so in a wet year the tree grew more than in a dry one. Actually, that's more difficult in that region than in colder climates, because there's a wider range of tree species. However, they did find a type of conifer which can live for over a thousand years, and that gave them the data they wanted: Vietnam and Thailand had experienced a severe drought in the early 1400s. So that suggests, though of course this can't be proved, that Angkor's decline was caused by its canals and reservoirs drying up, not by an invasion.

Appendix 6: A brief introduction to climate change

Defining climate change

'Climate' is not 'weather'. Weather can be understood to mean local or regional features of the atmospheric environment, which are short-term and temporary. Climate, on the other hand, is the general pattern of atmospheric or weather conditions in a local or regional area, or even of the Earth as a whole. As such, it is a long-term trend in weather conditions. Climate change occurs when this long-term pattern of weather and atmospheric conditions changes for some reason. It may be that particular features of the climate become different, such as increased rainfall, or temperature changes at different times of the year, but it could also mean that regions which once had stable weather slowly change to have highly varied and unpredictable weather patterns, and vice versa.

How does climate change differ from global warming?

The terms 'climate change' and 'global warming' are often misunderstood to mean the same thing. Indeed, people have tended to use them interchangeably to describe what many believe is an environmental crisis on 21st-century Earth. However, there are important differences between the two phenomena. Global warming refers specifically to increases in the average surface temperature of the planet as a whole. While it is certainly true that an increase in temperature of this sort will result in the climate changing, it is not the same thing. Climate change is the general alteration of climate, and while this includes temperature, it also covers changes in weather patterns such as precipitation and wind. The Earth's atmosphere and climate is a highly complex system, and it is impossible to predict accurately how different regions will be affected by global warming. As the planet warms overall, it may well cause different changes to the climate in different parts of the globe. Areas which previously enjoyed mild climates may become hotter, while some areas may in fact cool down.

Identifying the main causes of climate change

Climate change has been a natural feature of the Earth since long before the appearance of humans. In general, the climate of the Earth responds to the amount of the sun's energy which the planet absorbs or retains, and a change in either the amount of energy received or retained will cause the climate to change. At the most general level, climate change can be caused by a change in the amount of solar energy which is absorbed by the planet, both in its ground and sea surface, as well as the atmosphere. Scientists have identified natural 'solar cycles', where the output of solar energy shifts between warm and cool phases over vast timescales, leading to corresponding changes in atmospheric and surface temperatures on Earth. We are currently in the warm phase of one of these grand cycles.

Another general cause of climate change can be when something changes the amount of heat energy which the planet retains. Over a long period of time, the energy that the planet receives can escape back into space. This process helps to keep the average temperature and climate of the planet in balance. If, however, the heat energy becomes trapped inside the atmosphere, it will result in changes in weather conditions associated with an increase in overall temperature.

As well as changes caused by the natural solar cycle, the climate can be changed from within the atmosphere by such things as volcanic eruptions which release sulphur particles into the atmosphere, effectively blocking the amount of energy received from the sun, and geologic shifts which take place over vast periods of time.

However, besides natural causes there is also increasing evidence that human activity can result in climate change. So-called greenhouse gases, produced by industry and modern lifestyles, are one of the reasons why solar heat energy may be stopped from escaping into space. As we change the surface of the Earth we can also contribute to climate change by altering the balance of heat energy absorbed or retained by the planet.

The greenhouse effect

The greenhouse effect is the system by which the Earth regulates its own temperature, particularly keeping the planet warm enough for human, animal and plant life to survive. The greenhouse effect has been named after the manner in which farmers and gardeners can artificially create higher temperatures to nurture their plants by trapping heat inside glass. In the same way, the atmosphere, and the mix of particles and gases that it contains, traps the sun's heat near the Earth's surface. The sun's energy at first warms the surface of the Earth, and then, as the planet warms, it emits some of the heat energy back towards space as radiation. As the heat escapes back towards space, particles in the atmosphere, such as clouds or certain gases, absorb some of the heat and prevent it escaping. The system is evenly balanced, allowing just the right amount of heat to escape back into space to avoid disastrous overheating. There is a tendency to think that the greenhouse effect is a negative result of human release of industrial gases, but in fact it is an essential and entirely natural process, without which the Earth would be far too cold for almost anything to survive. However, human activity can enhance the greenhouse effect, emitting more gases and particles into the atmosphere which prevent heat escaping into space, and thereby warming the planet.

Are all greenhouse gases man-made?

A lot of people imagine that greenhouse gases are confined to the products of human industrial processes. They correctly identify certain gases created by human activity like CO_2, generated by fossil fuel use, nitrous oxide found in agricultural chemicals, and methane, released by farm livestock and the burning of vegetation. These are all significant contributors to climate change, with CO_2 being perhaps the most important. However, many people are surprised to learn that the most common greenhouse gas, if not the most damaging, is in fact water vapour. Water vapour in the atmosphere effectively absorbs heat energy which would otherwise be lost to space, and is a natural part of the greenhouse effect. However, a warming of the planet surface caused by human activities could also cause more water to evaporate into the air, thus increasing the overall amount of greenhouse gases beyond those directly emitted by humans.

Climate change – natural or man-made?

Until relatively recently there has been a spirited debate over climate change which centres around two main questions. Firstly, some people have questioned whether the Earth's climate is actually changing at all. In response to claims that the Earth's global average temperature is increasing, they have pointed to evidence which seems to show the opposite is true, for instance some glaciers around the world have actually increased in size, while other regions of the world have experienced cooler than average temperatures or seen once-moribund animal species revive spectacularly. A second question has been whether the change in climate, if it actually exists, is entirely natural, or is the result of human activity. The overwhelming amount of evidence which scientists have gathered over the last few decades now strongly suggests that the climate is changing, with the average global temperature increasing over the past 100 to 150 years, roughly the period since the start of the industrial revolution. Though there are some instances of glaciers increasing in size, the vast majority of the evidence points to polar ice caps and glaciers retreating, sea levels rising and a change in climatic regions. The period since 1980 has been the warmest on record. There is a growing consensus that climate change is a reality, even extending to people who had previously questioned its existence. However, some scientists and political leaders still claim that the change, while undeniable, is caused primarily by natural processes, and that the human influence is insignificant. Once again, though, there is a strong correlation between increased temperatures and human greenhouse gas emissions, and the consensus view is that there is a clear link between human activities and climate change.

The possible consequences of further climate change

Climate change will have consequences for both regional weather patterns and the human populations in different parts of the planet. These consequences will not simply be limited to higher temperatures, as many people suppose. Though the temperature of the planet as a whole is increasing, this will lead primarily to greater variation in weather patterns, as well as greater unpredictability in the type and intensity of weather phenomena. Changes in the environment caused by changes in the climate are likely to have profound effects upon the human population.

The planet's water is likely to be significantly affected by climate change. Melting ice caps will result in increasing sea levels, which are a particular threat to coastal communities and a large number of the world's major cities, which are built on coastal plains. Besides an increase in sea level, some areas are likely to experience a greater amount of flooding. Paradoxically, other areas will be more prone to drought, as rainfall decreases and rivers dry up or are over-exploited by humans. Political and military leaders are now taking scientists' warnings seriously, and preparing for conflicts over access to decreasing fresh water resources.

Changes in the climate are also likely to affect the planet's plant and animal life. Many species are only able to survive within a quite narrow band of climate and temperature conditions, and if these change, it can quickly result in the destruction of species and the habitats on which they depend. Large areas of tropical coral reef have been destroyed by increasing sea temperatures, which has a significant impact on the marine animals which depend on the reefs. Bee populations in Europe have been declining at an alarming rate, which is a particular threat to human food supplies because the bees play an important role in pollination of crops. Though there is no definitive proof as yet that the disappearance of bee colonies results directly from climate change, it is widely suspected that it is a consequence of human changes to the environment.

Climate change threatens human life and health. The incidence and severity of heat waves, periods of extreme high temperature, is increasing. In 2003, most of Europe experienced a severe heat wave which resulted in thousands of deaths across the continent, particularly in cities which trapped the heat and made it difficult to find relief. Besides the fatal consequences of heat waves, cities also suffer from increasingly poor air quality, disease and pest infestation, which threaten the health of their citizens.

Civil unrest and conflict also become more likely in a world where the certainties of a stable climate are disappearing. Climate change could cause once-fertile land to become barren, or destroy crops before harvest, resulting in a catastrophic lack of food. This in turn could lead to more of the sort of food riots that were seen around the world in 2008. Certain local conflicts have already been blamed on climate change.

Solving the problem of climate change

As the world warms, there is an increasingly urgent need to find and implement solutions to the climate change problem. So far most proposed solutions have fallen into two general categories: prevention and mitigation.

Most people are agreed that prevention would be the best solution to climate change. It is widely believed that if global CO_2 emissions can be reduced, then we will be able to prevent the Earth's temperature from rising to dangerous levels, and so prevent the disastrous consequences that would follow from that. Because CO_2 stays in the atmosphere for centuries after it is emitted, we know already that temperatures will continue to rise because of current and future CO_2 emissions, but there is a consensus opinion that the temperature rise should be limited to 2 °C in order to prevent the worst consequences of climate change.

Some climate change scientists, after analyzing the latest evidence, are beginning to claim that it is already too late to prevent temperatures rising by more than 2 °C. They hypothesize temperature increases of anywhere between 2 °C and 6 °C. The results of such an increase would almost certainly be disastrous, and so these scientists are calling not for prevention, which they believe is impossible, but mitigation of the worst effects. Mitigation means preparing for a world which will be significantly changed, and much more hostile to life. They advocate preparing strong defences against floods, enhanced agricultural techniques, hospitals, and emergency plans in order to prepare for such a future.

Whether prevention is still possible, or we must turn our efforts to mitigation, it is inevitable that some more warming will occur, and therefore perhaps it is necessary to prepare for the economic and social changes which are likely to result as we adapt to the changes in our climate. These changes will vary by region, depending on the way that the climate changes in each place. What is almost certain is that we will be required to make major changes to our way of life.

The international response to climate change

Though different regions will experience different consequences, climate change will affect the entire world, and therefore it is necessary that all nations attempt to reduce the greenhouse gas emissions. At the moment, the main focus on international efforts to deal with climate change is on prevention rather than mitigation. The 1997 Kyoto Protocol committed over 160 industrialized nations to reducing their greenhouse gas emissions, though some major industrial nations did not sign, and in fact most of the nations that did are not on course to meet their emissions targets.

The Intergovernmental Panel on Climate Change, established in 1988, reviews contributions made to the study of climate change from scientists across the globe, and provides regular updates of the extent of the problem. However, the IPCC's reports are not without controversy which has meant that not all nations have committed to the idea that they must act to prevent, or mitigate, climate change. Though there is a general scientific and political consensus that climate change exists and is a serious problem, the international response so far has shown that most governments are currently hesitant to make the far-reaching, and possibly economically damaging, changes that may be necessary.

Appendix 7: Recording script

Extract 1

Scientists are studying hundreds of DNA samples taken from people who have lived to the age of 100. They're hoping to find the genes that enable the long-lived to resist the diseases of ageing which affect the rest of the population. In a parallel breakthrough last week, researchers claimed that the physical health of ageing rats had been dramatically improved with a cocktail of ordinary dietary supplements such as vitamin and mineral pills, as though returning the rats to their younger state. Recently scientists were reported to have come their closest yet to discovering how to increase longevity. In experiments, fruit flies were given a drug which extended the normal lifespan of the flies by more than 50%.

These experiments seem to give hope that an elixir of life – a wonderful new way to improve the human lifespan – might soon be discovered. Unfortunately, the elixir of life in the form of a gene is, in reality, still a dream. A lifespan gene – responsible for controlling longevity – probably does not exist since there is no way for it to pass from one generation to another. It seems almost certain that people who reach the age of 100 or more do so actively, by avoiding disease, rather than by having a lucky gene for a long lifespan.

Extract 2

The search for long life may need to take a new path – one that leads away from genetics and cell biology and towards environmental factors such as diet. On the Japanese island of Okinawa, 457 people are more than 100 years old. That's about 35 100-year-old people for every 100,000 of the local population. Compare that with America, which has just ten 100-year-old people per 100,000 of the general population. So, why do Okinawans live such long and healthy lives? The answer undoubtedly lies not in their genes, but in the healthy food they eat and in their relatively stress-free and outdoor lifestyle.

The traditional Okinawan diet is heavy on rice, fish and vegetables and light on the dairy food which is so popular in America – red meat, eggs and milk, for example. An Okinawan proverb says that at 70 you are still a child, at 80 a young man or woman. And if at 90 someone from heaven invites you over, you should tell him: 'just go away and come back when I'm 100'. It is interesting that in another study it was found that breast cancer among Okinawan women is extremely rare, but that when these women emigrate to America and adopt a western diet heavy in dairy food, they begin to suffer breast cancer, and at the same high rates as American women. This clearly shows a link between diet, and the avoidance of a serious disease which can reduce lifespan.